RSC
Swan Theatre

An adaptation of

THE ROVER
(The Banished Cavaliers)

by Aphra Behn

A programme/text with commentary by Simon Trussler

D1348127

Swan Theatre Plays published by Methuen London
by arrangement with the Royal Shakespeare Company

methuen

Swan Theatre

The Swan Theatre is the newest of the Royal Shakespeare Company's five theatres but occupies that part of the original Shakespeare Memorial Theatre which survived the disastrous fire of 1926. The 800-seat Victorian Gothic Shakespeare Memorial Theatre, opened in 1879, had been built with funds raised in a national campaign led by local brewer Charles Edward Flower, who also generously donated the theatre's famous riverside site. In the years that followed its opening, Stratford-upon-Avon, long celebrated as Shakespeare's birthplace, also became a centre of Shakespearean performance.

Sir Frank Benson, who directed over thirty of the theatre's first fifty seasons, expressed his aims in 1905 in terms which remain relevant to today's Royal Shakespeare Company: 'to train a company, every member of which would be an essential part of a homogenous whole, consecrated to the practice of the dramatic arts and especially to the representation of the plays of Shakespeare'.

When, just a year after the granting, in 1925, of its Royal Charter, the theatre was almost completely destroyed by fire, a worldwide campaign was launched to build a new one. Productions moved to a local cinema until the new theatre, designed by Elisabeth Scott, was opened by the Prince of Wales on 23 April, 1932. Over the next thirty years, under the influence of directors such as Robert Atkins, Bridges-Adams, Iden Payne, Komisarjevsky, Sir Barry Jackson and Anthony Quayle, the Shakespeare Memorial Theatre maintained a worldwide reputation.

In 1960, the newly appointed artistic director, Peter Hall, extended the re-named Royal Shakespeare Company's operations to include a London base at the Aldwych Theatre, and widened the Company's repertoire to include modern as well as classical work. Other innovations of the period which have shaped today's Company were the travelling Theatregoround and experimental work which included the Theatre of Cruelty season.

Under Trevor Nunn, who took over as artistic director in 1968, this experimental work in small performance spaces led, in 1974, to the opening of The Other Place, Stratford-upon-Avon. This was a rehearsal space converted into a theatre and in 1977 its London counterpart, The Warehouse, opened with a policy of presenting new British plays. In the same year the RSC played its first season in Newcastle upon Tyne – now an annual event. In 1978, the year in which Terry Hands joined Trevor Nunn as artistic director, the RSC also fulfilled an ambition to tour to towns and villages with little or no access to live professional theatre.

In 1982, the RSC moved its London base to the Barbican Centre in the City of London, opening both the Barbican Theatre, specially built for the RSC by the generosity of the Corporation of the City of London, and The Pit, a small theatre converted like The Warehouse and The Other Place, from a rehearsal room.

Throughout its history, the RSC has augmented its central operations with national and international tours, films, television programmes, commercial transfers and fringe activities. Now, in the Swan Theatre, thanks to an extremely generous gift by an anonymous benefactor, the Company is able to explore the vast, popular output of Shakespeare's contemporaries and the period 1570-1750.

Despite box office figures, which, it is thought, have no equal anywhere in the world, the costs of RSC repertoire activities cannot be recouped from ticket sales alone. We rely on assistance from the Arts Council of Great Britain, amounting to about 40 per cent of our costs in any one year, from work in other media and, increasingly, on revenue from commercial sponsorship. To find out more about the RSC's activities and to make sure of priority booking for productions, why not become a member of the Company's Mailing List? For details of how to apply, please contact: Mailing List, Royal Shakespeare Theatre, Stratford-upon-Avon, Warwickshire CV37 6BB. Telephone: (0789) 205301.

RSC
Swan Theatre

CAST IN ORDER OF APPEARANCE

Belvile, *a Colonel* — **Hugh Quarshie**
Frederick, *his friend* } *four come out* — **Peter Guinness**
Blunt, *a country gull* } *of England* — **David Troughton**
Willmore, *the Rover* — **Jeremy Irons**
Lucetta, *a whore* — **Caroline Johnson**
Sancho, *her man* — **Tony Armatrading**
Florinda } — **Geraldine Fitzgerald**
Valeria } *three sisters* — **Lucy Hancock**
Hellena } — **Imogen Stubbs**
Don Pedro, *their brother* — **Nathaniel Parker**
Stephano } *his servants* — **Trevor Gordon**
Callis } — **Jenni George**
Angellica Bianca, *a famous courtesan* — **Sinead Cusack**
Moretta, *her woman* — **Rosalind Boxall**
Sebastian } *her bravos* — **Togo Igawa**
Biskey } — **Patrick Robinson**
Don Antonio, *the Viceroy's son* — **Philip Sully**
Diego, *his servant* — **Stan Pretty**
Phillip, *servant to the English* — **Brian Lawson**
Masquers/servants — **Tony Armatrading**
Jenni George
Trevor Gordon
Togo Igawa
Caroline Johnson
Brian Lawson
Stan Pretty
Patrick Robinson

Directed by — **John Barton**
Designed by — **Louise Belson**
Lighting by — **Wayne Dowdeswell**
Music by — **Guy Woolfenden**
Company voice work by — **Cicely Berry** and **David Carey**

Design Assistant — **Jill Jowett**
Stage Manager — **Michael Dembowicz**
Deputy Stage Manager — **Graham Watts**
Assistant Stage Manager — **Matthew Purves**

This performance is approximately 2 hours 45 minutes long including one interval of 20 minutes.

First performance of this RSC production, Swan Theatre, Stratford-upon-Avon, 3 July 1986

Please do not smoke or use cameras or tape recorders in the auditorium. And please remember that noise such as whispering, coughing, rustling programmes and the bleeping of digital watches can be distracting to performers and also spoils the performance for other members of the audience.

Arts Council Funded

RSC
Swan Theatre

Royal Shakespeare Company

Incorporated under Royal Charter as the
Royal Shakespeare Theatre
Patron Her Majesty The Queen
President Lord Wilson
Deputy President Sir Kenneth Cork
Chairman of the Council Geoffrey A Cass
Vice Chairman Dennis L Flower
Joint Artistic Directors Terry Hands Trevor Nunn
Direction Peggy Ashcroft John Barton Peter Brook
Terry Hands Trevor Nunn
Consultant Director Sir Peter Hall

Swan Theatre

Siobhan Bracke *Casting*
Wayne Dowdeswell *Chief Electrician*
Josie Horton *Deputy Wardrobe Mistress*
Geoff Locker *Production Manager*
Andy Matthews *Deputy Chief Electrician*
Philip Medcraft *Master Carpenter*
Janet Morrow *Publicity*
Nicola Russell *Press (0789) 296655*
Mo Weinstock *Sound*

Production Credits for The Rover

Scenery, costume and properties and wigs made in
RST workshops, Stratford-upon-Avon. Additional
costumes made by Kate Wyatt, Wallace &
McMurray, David Garret.
Production photographs by Donald Cooper.
Research by Leona Heimfeld.

Facilities

In addition to bar and coffee facilities on the
ground floor, there is wine on sale on the first floor
bridge outside Gallery 1. Toilets, including
facilities for disabled people, are situated on the
ground floor only.

RSC Collection

Each year the RSC Collection presents a theatre
exhibition associated with the season's plays. This
year's exhibition, to celebrate the opening of the
new Swan, concentrates on the changing styles of
staging from medieval times to the present day.
Come and see our exhibition; browse in the sales
and refreshments area – and book a backstage tour.

Swan Theatre Repertoire 1986

The Two Noble Kinsmen
by William Shakespeare
and John Fletcher

Every Man In His Humour
by Ben Jonson

The Rover
by Aphra Behn

From September
The Fair Maid of the West
by Thomas Heywood

Sponsored by

Stratford-upon-Avon
Herald

Contents

Director's Note, by John Barton 5

A Plan for the Swan, *by Trevor Nunn* 6

Sources and Stage History 7

Synopsis 7

Aphra Behn: a Brief Chronology 8

The Return of the Banished Cavaliers 9

The King, the Court, and the Courtesans 10

The Altered Face of the Stage 11

The Professionalism of Aphra Behn 12

The Sexual Economics of the Restoration 13

'The Injuries of Age and Time' 14

'The Rover' as Restoration Comedy 15

For Further Reading 16

The Rover 21

Director's Note

This is an adapted text, as established halfway through rehearsals. Further alterations will have been made to it before the production opened. About 550 lines have been cut and some 350 added.

Many of the new lines are taken from an earlier source play which Aphra Behn herself used extensively when she wrote *The Rover*. This is *Thomaso or The Wanderer* by Thomas Killigrew, published in 1664. Aphra Behn took over many of its situations, characters and lines, often word for word. Though *The Rover* is a far better play, it is hazy and loose in places, and *Thomaso* sometimes has the edge at specific moments.

The alterations I have made are partly to streamline our version and help to clarify a confusing plot. The most obvious change is the turning of Belvile into a black soldier of fortune, and the setting of the play in a Spanish colony rather than in Spain. I have however, deliberately avoided naming a specific location. The most obvious addition is that Valeria is introduced earlier in the action. Aphra Behn seems to regard her as an important engine of the plot, but does not have her speak until well into the play. The scene between Blunt and Lucetta is now closer to *Thomaso* than *The Rover*, Angellica's part has been expanded in the first half, as have the parts of Sebastian, Biskey and Sancho. And there are a number of substantial transpositions, particularly in the first four scenes.

John Barton
Stratford, May 1986

A Plan for the Swan

It was in the mid-seventies that an ambitious scheme was first put forward to convert the existing burnt-out shell of the old Shakespeare Memorial Theatre into the new Swan Theatre. It was not until the mid-eighties, however, that this dream of the RSC's Artistic Directorate was to become a reality with the inauguration of the Swan in April 1986 and the opening of The Two Noble Kinsmen. *In an early memorandum outlining a policy for the new theatre Trevor Nunn wrote:*

Since the idea of the Swan was first conceived, it was accompanied by the twin notion of what should be its repertoire. John Napier was first commissioned in 1978 to design an auditorium inside the shell of the Conference Hall: the architectural nature of the new theatre and the parameters of its repertoire were to be indivisible. Michael Reardon, the architect, is now in the process of fulfilling this original brief, and a custom-built theatre, in the most precise sense of the term, is nearing completion – a theatre for the performance of sixteenth, seventeenth and eighteenth-century plays which can be seen as broadly contextual to our house dramatist, William Shakespeare.

Since 1964 we had agreed that in an ideal world we should be doing one play a year by Shakespeare's contemporaries, and we did indeed produce in the main house *The Duchess of Malfi, Women Beware Women, The Jew of Malta, The Revenger's Tragedy* and *Dr Faustus.* However, the worsening overall financial position of the Company decreed that we could no longer afford the comparatively lower box-office response for the annual non-Shakespeare.

Naturally the inauguration of The Other Place provided us with a space for alternatives to Shakespeare, as much as for alternatives to the methods and values of the international cultural centre which the Royal Shakespeare Company had become. So, as a Company, we have almost continuously responded to the imperative of presenting examples of the plays which might have influenced Shakespeare, or the plays which he might have influenced, or the plays which give us, both practitioners and audiences, greater insight into sixteenth and seventeenth-century England.

In the process, we have revealed the existence of several minor masterpieces, we have discovered several exceptions to the 'genres' that scholars might have led us to expect, we have proved that 'neglected' works can still provide tremendous entertainment and theatrical excitement, and we have proved that Shakespeare was surrounded by approaches to dramaturgy which were almost certainly experimental and which can lay claim to being considered more modern and comprehensible to us than his own. And we have only scratched the surface.

There remain countless plays that have continued dormant and which deserve our attention. We have only touched the obvious Marlowe plays, we have never explored the Shakespeare apocrypha, and (bordering on disgrace) we have only ever attempted three plays by Ben Jonson, who in any other language would be the national playwright and have a theatre devoted to him. We have scarcely visited the sixteenth century before Shakespeare, we have never done a masque, and it is high time we tested received ideas about the Restoration, since there would seem to be at least as many exceptions as there are rules.

Of necessity, the key to the whole operation is that the interior design of the theatre amounts to a permanent staging. There is a promontory stage, and back wall that continues the galleried features of the auditorium to provide a sense of upper and inner stage, without amounting to an attempt to 'recreate' the Globe or even the original Swan. It is the simplest possible structure on which we can present the pre-proscenium plays of our dramatic tradition. It is a theatre for texts and actors, for the work of analysis, structure, insight and performance. Clearly, design will have a vital significance in what we do there, but it cannot be design involving changing the configuration of the stage, or even of 'set building' in the sense that we currently understand it.

The task is to prove that these plays live, not that they can be preserved in aspic. And in terms of the first few years at the Swan the task is to communicate and insist on the special identity of the theatre and its policy. So the very first year must not only observe the policy but expound and extol it.

I propose that we should do four plays. One from the Shakespeare apocrypha to establish the link with the main house and the contextual bearing; one early Elizabethan or pre-Shakespearean play to establish the breadth of the territory we are to investigate; one neglected classic from Shakespeare's Elizabethan or Jacobean contemporaries; and one play from the late-seventeenth or early-eighteenth century, to define the opposite bank.

Commentary
compiled by Simon Trussler

Sources and Stage History

In a postscript to the first edition of *The Rover*, published in 1677, Aphra Behn thought it necessary to defend herself against charges of plagiarism: but she made no secret of her debt to Thomas Killigrew's earlier play *Thomaso; or, The Wanderer*, which had been written without any expectation of performance during the interregnum, in 1654, and published in Killigrew's *Comedies and Tragedies* ten years later. Mrs. Behn claims that she might as well be accused of taking her ideas from Richard Brome's *The Novella*, first performed in 1632: but whereas she borrowed from Brome only in minor matters of construction, and perhaps for a faint original of her Angellica, *The Rover* is clearly obliged to Killigrew's play in its general plot outline, and there are also some stylistic echoes. A comparison of her Willmore and Ned Blunt with Killigrew's counterparts, Thomaso and Edwardo, however, shows how far her skill in characterization transcends her source, just as she is superior to the prolix Killigrew in sustaining the dramatic pace, and in her tightness of construction.

Like so many of Mrs. Behn's plays, *The Rover* was first performed in the Dorset Garden Theatre, which had been planned for the Duke of York's company under Davenant, but was opened after his death with Thomas Betterton as joint manager in 1671. The first recorded performance of the play was on 24 March 1677, when Charles II was present to see Betterton take the role of Belvile, with his wife Mary as Florinda. Betterton's friend, the versatile actor William Smith, played Willmore, and the brilliant low comedian Cave Underhill took the part of Ned Blunt. Elizabeth Barry, who was to become better known for her tragic roles, played Hellena, and Anne Quin was Angellica.

Although the play was revived every few years until the turn of the century – at least in 1680, 1685, and 1696, sometimes at royal command – it was in the first half of the eighteenth century that it became firmly established in the repertoire, from which it was absent for only a single season between 1703 and 1743. Following in the footsteps of Will Mountfort's Willmore – 'dangerous to see', according to Queen Mary, because 'he made vice so alluring' – Robert Wilks often took the role early in the new century, although Verbruggen, Ryan, and Giffard were also seen in the part. Among the many Hellenas were Mrs. Verbruggen, Anne Oldfield, Mrs. Mountfort, Mrs. Rogers, Mrs. Bradshaw, Mrs. Bullock, Mrs. Bracegirdle, Mrs Vincent, and later Peg Woffington. Mrs. Barry had graduated to Angellica by 1707.

A revival at Covent Garden in 1757 – with Ned Shuter following in the footsteps of Estcourt, Penkethman, and Theophilus Cibber to make an outstanding Blunt – led to further productions in the following four seasons, but the play then disappeared from the repertoire until 1790, when an adaptation entitled *Love in Many Masks* was put together by Kemble for Drury Lane. The need for his tasteful but debilitating bowdlerisation sufficiently suggests why the stage history of *The Rover* was then interrupted for the best part of two hundred years.

Synopsis

'The rover' is the philandering cavalier Willmore, a naval adventurer who meets up with his fellow exiles from Cromwell's rule – the mercenary soldiers Belvile and Frederick, and the rustic gull Ned Blunt – in a Spanish colony, as the pre-Lenten carnival is about to begin. The eldest of three sisters, Florinda, is in love with Belvile, but is intended by her father to marry an elderly suitor, and by her brother Don Pedro for his own friend, the viceroy's son Don Antonio. The sprightly Hellena, reluctantly preparing to take the veil, and the demure but calculating Valeria plan with her to disguise themselves, join in the celebrations, and look out for men.

Antonio and Pedro fall out over the charms of the courtesan Angellica, who is demanding an outrageous thousand crowns for her favours; but she is eventually seduced into giving them gratis to the flamboyant but impoverished Willmore, of whom she becomes wildly jealous when she catches him later paying court to Hellena, in her gypsy disguise. Florinda has meanwhile arranged a midnight meeting with Belvile at her garden gate, but before his arrival she is accosted by the drunken Willmore, who disturbs the whole house.

As Belvile reproaches his friend, they observe Antonio about to enter Angellica's house, and Willmore wounds his rival – but it is Belvile who is arrested. Belvile is brought before Don Antonio, who resigns his own interest in Florinda to him in return for Belvile agreeing to stand in for Antonio in the duel planned with Don Pedro. Belvile almost gets possession of his mistress as a result, but is thwarted yet again by the untimely arrival of Willmore.

Hellena now fans the flames of jealousy between Angellica and Willmore, while Florinda, fleeing from her brother, finds herself in the hands of Ned Blunt – intent on avenging himself against women for the trick by which the prostitute Lucetta has deprived him of his possessions and his dignity. But his friends arrive in time to prevent a rape, Florinda's identity is discovered, and she and Belvile secure a priest to marry them, of whose services Valeria and Frederick also take advantage. Willmore is rescued by Antonio from death at the hands of the vengeful Angellica, but not from marriage at the hands of Hellena. Don Pedro reluctantly resigns himself to events.

Aphra Behn: a Brief Chronology

1640   *c.* Born, conjecturally in early July, at Wye or Sturry, near Canterbury, Kent. Maiden name Amies, Johnson, or Cooper.

1663   *c.* Family in Surinam, but her father, who had been appointed Lieutenant-General, died on the voyage. Stayed on a local plantation.

1664   Returned to London in the spring. Presented an Indian costume to the King's Company.

1665   *c.* Marriage to Mr. Behn, probably a Dutch merchant, who died soon afterwards, perhaps during the Great Plague.

1666   Persuaded by Thomas Killigrew to serve as a spy in the Dutch Wars, but discovered little of value while in Antwerp, and remained unpaid for her services. Great Fire of London in her absence.

1667   Returned to London.

1668   Committed to prison for debt, despite petitions to Killigrew and the King. Date of release uncertain.

1670   Beginning of her career as a professional writer. December, her first play, the tragi-comic *The Forced Marriage*, performed by the Duke's Company at Lincoln's Inn Fields, with Betterton in the lead, achieving a run of six nights. Around this time, beginning of her long relationship with the dissolute lawyer John Hoyle.

1671   Her second tragi-comedy, *The Amorous Prince*, at Lincoln's Inn Fields in the spring.

1672   Possibly edited the collection of poetry, *The Covent-Garden Drollery*.

1673   Feb., failure of her comedy of intrigue *The Dutch Lover* at Dorset Garden.

1676   The passionate tragedy *Abdelazer* performed at Dorset Garden in July, followed there in September by a 'scandalous' comedy with brothel scenes, *The Town Fop*.

1677   March, *The Rover* produced at Dorset Garden. Two other plays attributed to her also seen at Dorset Garden, *The Debauchee* in February and *The Counterfeit Bridegroom* in September.

1678   January, *Sir Patient Fancy*, a comedy adapted from Molière's *The Imaginary Invalid*, at Dorset Garden. The Popish Plot 'revealed' by Titus Oates.

1679   Beginning of the exclusion crisis. The comedy *The Feigned Courtesans* seen in the spring, and the tragi-comedy *The Young King* in early autumn, both at Dorset Garden.

1680   Death of John Wilmot, Earl of Rochester, aged 33.

1681   April, *The Second Part of The Rover*; November, the farcical comedy *The False Count*; and December, the historical comedy *The Roundheads:* all at Dorset Garden.

1682   The anti-Whig political lampoon *The City Heiress* 'well-received' at Dorset Garden in the spring, but *Like Father, Like Son* which failed there, remained unprinted, and is now lost apart from prologue and epilogue. Increasing hostility from the Whigs leads to her arrest for the 'abusive' and 'scandalous' prologue she contributed in August to the anonymous *Romulus and Hersilia*: she was probably let off with a caution. Merging of the two theatre companies.

1683   Wrote three of her posthumously-published short novels, and the first part of *Love Letters between a Nobleman and His Sister*.

1684   Published her *Poems on Several Occasions*.

1685   Publication of her poetic *Miscellany*. Death of Charles II and accession of his brother James II.

1686   The prose work *La Montre; or, The Lover's Watch* published. Returned to the theatre in April with the comedy *The Lucky Chance* at Drury Lane.

1687   The *commedia*-style farce *The Emperor of the Moon*, one of her greatest successes, first seen at Drury Lane in March. Arrest and inconclusive trial of John Hoyle for sodomy.

1688   Published the short novels *The Fair Jilt*, *Agnes de Castro*, and *Oroonoko*, the latter based on her experiences in Surinam. The 'bloodless revolution' leads to the abdication of James II, and the protestant supremacy under William and Mary.

1689   16 April, died, and buried in Westminster Abbey. Posthumous production in November of her last play, the comedy *The Widow Ranter* at Drury Lane, a failure. The comedy *The Younger Brother* also first produced posthumously, at Drury Lane in February 1696.

> 'The wit of her comedies seems to be generally acknowledged, and it is equally acknowledged that they are very indecent, on which account I have not thought myself under any obligation to peruse them. It would have been an unworthy employment, nicely to estimate a wit which, having been applied to the purposes of impiety and vice, ought not only to be held in the utmost detestation, but consigned, if possible, to eternal oblivion.'
>
> *Dr. Kippis (1778)*

The Return of the Banished Cavaliers

The events which restored Charles II to the English throne in May 1660 were fast-moving: as late as September 1659, both Charles and his brother James had appeared to be making plans for an indefinite exile. Much had to be done during the new king's 'honeymoon' with his people, and it is a measure of the importance attached by Charles to theatrical matters that he seems to have given no less urgent attention to sorting out the squabbles between the various entrepreneurs vying to form new theatrical companies than to reconciling the old enemies of the civil war.

Exile for Charles had been, after his apparently final defeat at Worcester in 1651, a relatively comfortable affair, passed mainly in the civilised if often conspiratorial surroundings of Paris and Brussels: but for many of the followers of the king and his 'martyred' father, the interregnum was spent in a constant struggle against hardship. Some laid low at home, their estates confiscated or sold off piecemeal to meet fines for their 'delinquency'. Others, like Belvile and Willmore in *The Rover*, turned soldiers or sailors of fortune, accumulating mistresses, booty, or battle honours with an equally casual loyalty.

Most of the young Restoration gallants, now returning along with their king, would thus in all probability have spent a childhood or adolescence in the turbulent atmosphere of civil war, the early years of their adult life cut off from family traditions and that sense of service which possession of land could still, on occasion, encourage. Nor did the Restoration settlement return the estates sold off by persecuted royalists to 'upstart' puritan landgrabbers. Lacking roots, but often bearing a load of such grudges, these 'rovers' saw little reason not to pursue in England the kind of desperate sexual and economic opportunism which had become habitual – and was now also reflected in the theatre to which they flocked.

Besides, there was even a sort of theological justification for living out the belief that 'debauchery was loyalty, gravity rebellion'. Anything that inverted the detested values of puritanism had its own validity – and, as it happened, an open delight in sexual dalliance (as in theatricality) happened to coincide with the tastes of the restored monarch. No wonder that Charles's court in Whitehall proved such a magnet, and that its values so permeated the life and attitudes of 'the town' – which, it should be remembered, meant the fashionable residential and shopping area of which Covent Garden was the heart and the Strand the main artery, as distinct from 'the city', whose tradesmen and financiers, tainted with puritan sympathies, became the 'cits' so often mocked in the prologues, epilogues, and cuckoldings of Restoration comedy.

That the king no less than his courtiers were often dependent on the financial assistance of such people made it, of course, all the more necessary to display them as semi-illiterate upstarts in the theatre – which they nevertheless also attended, sometimes in such numbers as to spoil Samuel Pepys's enjoyment. The tensions of a nation and a capital which remained so divided were reflected in the microcosmic conditions of its theatre: and although the ostensible world of *The Rover* is that of exile in a faraway country, its values are those of men restored to their country, but not to their own.

The thwarting of an aged father's wish to marry his daughter to a rich but geriatric suitor is an age-old theme of comedy: but whereas the contemporary *commedia* made prominent characters of its Pantaloons and their doddering friends, it is significant that Mrs. Behn keeps Florinda's stern father and the farting Don Vincentio permanently off-stage. The traditional struggles between the values of youth and age, poverty and wealth, give way here to just the kind of internecine, sexual warfare through which the 'banished cavaliers' of real life continued to forget – or to sublimate – their sorrows.

'From Aphra Behn's point of view *The Rover* was her most outright and positive celebration of those cavalier childhood heroes. Here with the 'masculine' part of her, her poetry as she was to describe it in the preface to *The Lucky Chance*, she could be one of them at last. But as the writer is rarely just one person among a fictitious crowd so I believe, though her identification with the cavaliers is intense, that she was at the same time AB, the courtesan Angellica Bianca. Her trade was words, and it was impossible that she shouldn't have noticed those initials. Perhaps that was why she chose [Killigrew's] play.'

Maureen Duffy (1977)

'For Aphra Behn, writing was an act of sexual politics, a balancing of the powers of "masculine" intellect and "feminine" charm (as intellect and charm were conceived of as gendered subjects in the seventeenth century) in a daring leap toward freedom of speech and action for women. She was principally concerned with what might be called the public and private faces of women's oppression in the society of seventeenth-century England. Contemporary marriage customs which forced women into marriage for lack of any other recourse represented the public face of the oppression; the private face was the unspoken distrust of and prejudice against women writers.'

Cheri Davis Langdell (1985)

The King, the Court, and the Courtesans

The character of Charles II might very easily have been conceived as the hero of a Wycherley play – dour, cynical, and introverted at heart, yet capable of a pretty wit, and sexually attractive beyond the advantages of *force majeure*. Whether his personality was shaped by exile, or simply well-adapted to it, the fact remains that, before the Restoration, Charles enjoyed the semblance of both power and responsibility without the reality of either: life became, in short, a form of playacting. Later, when the king strolled, supposedly incognito but recognised by all, into the House of Lords to listen to a debate, he would duly declare the entertainment as good as a play, and sardonically join in the laughter at veiled references to himself.

In exile, Charles had pursued his women with no less fervour then Willmore or Belvile in *The Rover*. The shadow cast over his marriagability by the attempts of one of his early mistresses, Lucy Walter, to declare herself his lawful wife ironically allowed him all the more freedom to engage in other affairs, for which he sought among his own camp-followers, the nobility of the French court, and the brothels of Paris with a fine impartiality which led one of his recent biographers, J.P. Kenyon, to describe him as 'not a gourmet so much as a gourmand' in sexual matters.

Back home, Charles's male companions were drawn largely from a promiscuous, hard-drinking, but highly-literate set which included, besides the notorious Earl of Rochester, the Duke of Buckingham, Sir George Etherege, and Charles Sedley – all playwrights, as much probably from fashion as inspiration, just as in other ages courtiers might have been concerned to excel at hunting deer, jousting, or grouse-shooting. These were men to whom casual violence came readily, and who walked that uneasy tightrope between rape and seduction, or between brutality and the defence of honour, which is so often reflected in the plays they wrote and watched. A regular attender at the theatres, Charles himself is said to have lent a hand in the writing of plays, and he also interested himself in matters of casting. He both encouraged and emulated the Restoration 'style', in dramatic art as in life – and apparently displayed it as freely among women of good breeding as among his male cronies or his concubines. It made for sexual equality, of a sort.

When the dynastic imperative finally cornered the king into marriage, he took to wife the unfortunate princess Catherine of Braganza – in part to safeguard the alliance with her native Portugal, in part to produce for him an unquestionably legitimate heir. This, perhaps by way of unconscious vengeance, she resolutely failed to do – so perpetuating the long drawn-out crisis over the ever-likelier succession of Charles's Catholic brother, James. The king's treatment of his wife in many ways epitomised the double standards of Restoration comedy. In private, he humiliated her by appointing his own mistresses – successively, Barbara Villiers, Countess of Castlemaine, and Louise de Kéroualle, Duchess of Portsmouth – as ladies of her bedchamber. Yet in public his curious sense of honour combined with his political instinct, and when the Whigs backed Titus Oates's allegations of Catherine's complicity in a plot to poison her husband, they misjudged their man. Charles refused to put away his wife, the allegations collapsed – and the Whigs, by then espousing the cause of Charles's illegitimate son, Monmouth, lost all credibility, along with their hopes of excluding James from the succession.

Mrs. Behn flayed the Whigs with impunity in *The City Heiress* in 1682, but when she extended her target to include Monmouth himself, in the sniping prologue she contributed to *Romulus and Hersilia* later that year, she was arrested, and at least severely reprimanded. Charles's affection for his unruly bastard son, or some perverse sense of his far-flung family's dignity, never entirely deserted him – nor, of course, did he forget his mistresses, of whom two of the most prominent came from the theatre. Mary Davis he took from the Duke's company, and the almost legendary Nell Gwyn from the King's – where her position was due to real talent and wit as well as to her undoubted beauty. When her coach was mistaken for the Catholic Duchess of Portsmouth's at the height of the exclusion crisis, Nell entirely won over a jostling mob by declaring from the window, 'Pray, good people, be civil. I am the *protestant* whore!' The line displays all the wry, self-aware sexuality of one of Aphra Behn's new women. The two were, in fact, close friends.

Even in death, Charles exhibited something like the last-act repentance of a rake from Restoration comedy: at the prompting of Lady Portsmouth, he was attended by a priest, and made a deathbed conversion to Catholicism – the priest, by a fine irony, taking the covert, backstairs route to his bedchamber well-worn by so many of Charles's mistresses. And among his last words were those of commendation to his brother James: 'Let not poor Nelly starve.' In a room filled with as many illegitimate offspring as could be hastily assembled, neither Nell Gwyn nor any of his other women were permitted to pay their last respects. Poor Nelly, as it happened, died of an apoplexy soon after, but the Duchess of Mazarin lived on, through reaction and revolution, to die still in receipt of a royal pension in 1699. There is little in Restoration comedy which exceeds Charles's personal excesses, or typifies better than his own conduct the mixture of calculation and generosity – and the downright double-standards – which characterised the Restoration 'wit'.

The Altered Face of the Stage

'They altered at once the whole face of the stage by introducing scenes and women' – or so John Dennis claimed nostalgically, writing in 1725 of the events of 1660, when play-acting was once more permitted after being banned by the puritans since 1642. The court masques of the Jacobean and Caroline theatre had, it's true, employed quite elaborate scenery, and the open-air theatres of the Elizabethans had long been giving way to indoor 'private' theatres, with greater potential for technical effects. The difference now was that the proscenium arch formed a 'picture-frame' for the painted perspective scenery, changed by the wings-and-shutters system, which provided a formalised background to Restoration comedy and tragedy.

But it was *only* a background: the actors performed on the extensive apron stage in front of the proscenium, in a relationship with their audiences no less intimate and uncluttered than their forebears. Indeed, Restoration theatres, which seated from around five to eight hundred, were actually smaller than the Elizabethan public playhouses, and their audiences, although not drawn quite so exclusively from a courtly elite as has sometimes been suggested, certainly felt themselves to be part of a social as much as a theatrical occasion.

Quite how that 'crossing of the boundary' between actor and character, so clearly felt in Restoration prologues and epilogues, affected the acting of the play itself is not certain: but the style would certainly have been presentational rather than realistic – at a time, confessedly, when rituals of 'presentation' were of great importance to everyday behaviour as well. So, with directors unthought of, and playwrights far less involved in the practical business of mounting a play than their Elizabethan counterparts, the influence of the dancing-master was probably strong in matters of movement and stage grouping. As Jocelyn Powell has aptly summed it up: 'The atmosphere of the Restoration theatre was that of a sophisticated cabaret.'

Of those bidding for the right to build their own companies amidst the political confusion of Charles's return, the successful 'patentees' were both men of influence at court, who had had experience of theatre before the civil wars. It was Thomas Killigrew who wrote the play on which Mrs. Behn based *The Rover* – but whereas his *Thomaso* had been intended for reading only, Sir William Davenant had even succeeded in getting plays with music produced under Cromwell's guard (so that English opera, as later with melodrama, began as a means of getting round the law). Davenant was given his royal patent to manage, under the patronage of the Duke of York, a company which first played in a converted 'real' tennis court at Lincoln's Inn Fields, and which moved in 1671 to Wren's Dorset Garden Theatre beside the Thames, where so many of Mrs. Behn's plays were performed. Killigrew's company, which came under the king's own patronage, played in another converted tennis court until the first Drury Lane Theatre was completed in 1663, to be replaced by a new playhouse in 1674 after its destruction by fire.

With just two companies of less than thirty players apiece – reduced to the single 'united' company from 1682 to 1695 – acting was thus an exclusive though not prestigious profession, its members as well-known personally to many in the audience as their own acquaintances in the pit or boxes. And, although the patents stressed that the introduction of actresses was a matter of morality – to correct the abuse of men appearing 'in the habits of women' – intimacy between these players and their audiences was not confined to closeness in the auditorium. It was probably inevitable that, in the absence of a traditional route for women into the profession, some actresses in a licentious age should have achieved their positions through sexual patronage – though it's also indisputable that Elizabeth Barry, despite her path being smoothed by the notorious rake Lord Rochester, became a truly great tragic actress, while Nell Gwyn, although she owed her early chances to being the mistress of a leading player, Charles Hart, became no less striking a comic actress before she caught the eye of the king.

Other actresses, such as the great Thomas Betterton's wife Mary, were nonetheless able to lead lives of untained virtue at a time when such behaviour in courtly society was almost eccentric – while the fine comic actress Anne Bracegirdle even managed to sustain a reputation for excessive prudishness in private life. This did not, however, prevent her being thought fair game for predatory males: as late as 1692, an assault on her honour was compounded by the murder of the actor William Mountford, who had tried to intervene on her behalf. Those guilty were not severely punished.

This was an age when Rochester might order Dryden to be beaten up in a back alley for an imagined satirical slight; when the king himself could instigate an assault upon a parliamentarian who had dared to criticise his mistresses; and when Rochester and Sedley could attempt the rape of an heiress in broad daylight. The mixture of violence and casual sexuality which Aphra Behn presents even less discreetly than most of her contemporaries is thus a reflection on the stage of the very brittle veneer of politeness which barely concealed the viciousness of much high-society life.

The Professionalism of Aphra Behn

Aphra Behn was not the first woman playwright: that distinction goes, curiously, to a tenth-century Benedictine nun named Hrotsvitha, who wrote six religious dramas while in the German abbey of Gandersheim. That Hrotsvitha's plays should glorify the virtue of chastity was only to be expected in a period when the typology of women allowed few gradations between the virgin and the whore, other than that of the nagging shrew – but it makes a wry contrast to the approach of her Restoration successors in the craft.

Mrs. Behn was not quite the earliest of these. The Marchioness of Newcastle published two collections, including some twenty plays, in 1662 and 1668, but these were purely 'closet dramas', and never performed. Catherine Phillips, however, achieved the honour of having her *Pompey*, a version of Corneille's play, performed in the brand new Smock Alley Theatre in Dublin in February 1663 – and so of inaugurating the vogue for 'heroic dramas', in the rhymed couplets which were to displace blank verse as the main medium for tragic writing until Buckingham's *The Rehearsal* helped to burlesque heroics off the stage in 1671.

Just as Catherine Phillips adopted the pen-name of Orinda, so Aphra Behn also allowed herself to be known as Astraea. But Mrs. Phillips had written purely for her own amusement, at a time when most male playwrights were courtiers and men of letters, often unconcerned with the income their plays produced – whereas Aphra Behn wrote from pressing financial need. The theatre of the period differed from Shakespeare's in that most playwrights were not formally attached to a particular company. Dryden's contract to write three plays a year in return for becoming a 'sharer' in the King's company was unusual – and unfulfilled. Generally, the professional writer was dependent upon the benefit system, whereby the profits of the third night's performance – and perhaps of the sixth, and very exceptionally of the ninth – were allocated to him. A good benefit could reap as much as £100, with a further lump sum possible for publication: but there was no guarantee that any play would even reach the third night, and it was thus as important that a sympathetic audience should give a good reception on the first night, as that a rich one (perhaps willing to make presents over the odds) should fill the house on the third.

Those males scandalised by Mrs. Behn, who dared to affront 'the modesty of her sex' by writing as bawdily as they, did not even deign to consider the element of economic necessity that drove her to satisfy the prevailing tastes of the town. She was among the more prolific of Restoration playwrights in part because she *had* to be – and the total of at least sixteen plays performed during her lifetime is thus in marked contrast with, say, Wycherley's four, or Congreve's six. When she declared in the preface to her late comedy *The Lucky Chance* (1686) that she was 'not content to write for a third night only', she may simply have been staking a claim to be writing for posterity as well as for money: but her invariable association with Dorset Garden from 1673 until the merging of the companies in 1682 may suggest some more formal arrangement with the Duke's company than the chances of the benefit system allowed.

The merger of the companies was a consequence of the decline in theatre attendances in the wake of the political crises of Charles's later years; and the United Company cut its costs still further by including a higher proportion of revivals, whose dead authors made no claim upon diminishing receipts. Other playwrights, such as Aphra's friends Thomas Otway and William Wycherley, fared no better, and John Dryden was forced to seek meagre government patronage. Classically-educated males could at least turn to publishing translations as an alternative source of income – whereas Mrs. Behn, in contributing to a version of Ovid, had to work from a literal first draft. Greek and Latin were no part of expected female 'accomplishments'.

Aphra Behn enjoyed renewed stage success in later life – notably with *The Lucky Chance* and the strikingly original *The Emperor of the Moon*. But increasingly – and in not dissimilar circumstances to her eighteenth-century successor, Henry Fielding – she turned from plays to writing novels. In 1688, the year before her death, she published *Oroonoko*, the work by which she probably remains best known – its anti-slavery theme anticipating Harriet Beecher Stowe, and its element of noble savagery even upstaging Rousseau. Whether or not she was the first 'true' novelist, before such aspirants as Defoe, Richardson, and Fielding himself, depends on one's definition of the form – a form in which, however, later women writers were to challenge masculine 'supremacy' with far greater success than, Aphra Behn excepted, they ever challenged male chauvinism in the theatre.

'With Mrs. Behn . . . we come to town and rub shoulders with ordinary people in the streets. Mrs. Behn was a middle-class woman with all the plebeian virtues of humour, vitality, and courage; a woman forced by the death of her husband and some unfortunate adventures of her own to make her living by her wits. She made, by working very hard, enough to live on. The importance of that fact outweighs anything she actually wrote. . . . For now that Aphra Behn had done it, girls could go to their parents and say, You need not give me an allowance; I can make money by my pen. Of course the answer for many years to come was, Yes, by living the life of Aphra Behn! Death would be better! and the door was slammed faster than ever.'

Virginia Woolf (1929)

The Sexual Economics of the Restoration

Charles Dickens may not actually have invented 'the values of family life' along with the traditional English Christmas, but it's undeniable that in much pre-romantic drama and literature there's little love lost between fathers and sons, elder and younger brothers, or husbands and wives. The death of a wealthy father or elder brother is more usually a matter for congratulation among the friends of the fortunate heir – while marriage, of course, has everything to do with the businesslike arrangement of property and dynasties, and very little to do with the affections.

True love, before marriage or after, is reserved for a mistress – though in most romantic comedies, where love is actually permitted to lead towards marriage, the hopeful suitor is usually assured, by luck or judgement, of a respectable fortune besides. In real life, the young couple might not even have met before their parents or go-betweens had finished arranging the match. (Ordinary working folk could, ironically, better 'afford' to marry for love the less they could afford anything else: but, until quite recently, ordinary working folk have not much figured in great literature or theatre, other than as comic relief.)

The matter is further complicated by the 'sexual revolution' which led Charles I to declare in 1664 that 'the passion of love is very much out of fashion in this country'. Even the once-adored mistress was now regarded as for sexual satisfaction only – an object of that curious combination of arousal and disgust which permeates the poems of such burnt-out rakes as Rochester. And the disgust is perhaps most readily heaped on those women who tried reciprocally to exercise the sexual freedom they had supposedly been granted.

In herself advocating a more liberal sexuality for women, Aphra Behn acknowledged, too, that the lack of an equivalent economic independence, combined with the fear or actuality of childbirth and the earlier loss of physical charms, constrained women from exercising their 'freedom' from a position of any other equality than that of their wits. And freedom of sexual movement was not freedom of *social* movement: the over-compliant mistress was still widely regarded as no better than a whore – to which status abandonment or decline could all too often reduce her. Mrs. Behn herself enjoyed the relative independence from male domination that only widowhood could bring – but not the inherited fortune that would have added security to freedom. If Restoration actresses also called themselves 'Mrs.' it was not because they had all been married, but because 'Miss' had come to be suggestive merely of sexual availability.

Aphra Behn was not above evading the problem in her plays – or rather, not above reconciling it as many writers had done and would do again, by such a device as she used in *The Dutch Lover*, where, for all her heroine's vaunted rebellion against paternal choice, her self-selected lover turns out to be her father's preferred suitor as well. And if the very title of her first play, *The Forced Marriage*, anticipates the importance of the theme to her writing, by her second, *The Amorous Prince*, she was falling back on the convention that the most promiscuous rake allows himself to be reformed in time for the final curtain.

The Town Fop showed the horrific consequences of a forced marriage, from which the participants are only released thanks to the hero's earlier, legally-binding pledge of marriage to his mistress. The father, meanwhile, has had time to see the awful consequences of his preferred alliance – which include the hero spending half his unwanted wife's portion on a wild debauch. But no resolution is offered by Mrs. Behn to the economic and sexual plight of that rejected wife – a 'loose end' not dissimilar to that in *The Rover* of the scorned Angellica, in whom the playwright seems to have invested a considerable, perhaps all too personal passion.

Aphra Behn, then, made no pretence of having resolved, dramatically or personally, all the problems posed by the combination of new attitudes to sexuality with very old attitudes to other kinds of freedom. In many ways she was no less equivocal or downright muddled about sex than most of her male counterparts – though she probably did recognise, along with her recent biographer Angeline Goreau, that the 'liberated' wits of the Restoration were fearfully if unconsciously obsessed with 'the possibility that women might have sexual desires that were independent of their role as passive receptacles of male desire'.

That Hellena in *The Rover* falls in love with Willmore for all the wrong reasons may tell us more about Aphra Behn's own unfortunate liaisons than about Hellena: but neither the character nor her creator was a 'passive receptacle'. What Behn did achieve, in her writing if not perhaps in her life, was a triumphant assertion of women's rights to their own sexuality, and at least the tentative expression – if her plays were to remain commercial, it could be no more than tentative – of her belief that true sexual satisfaction for both men *and* women lay in close and reciprocal relationships, not in the yoking of sexuality to property rights and family trees.

'Her very writing and her attitude toward it are acts of sexual politics. As practised by Behn's women characters and by Behn and other women playwrights of the Restoration . . . sexual politics was woman's resourceful exertion of whatever power she may have – sexual, social, economic, or political – so as to redress the social and psychosexual balance ever so slightly in her favour. If in Kate Millett's conception of sexual politics the term implies male domination of women in their sexual roles, in feminist and female writers of the Restoration sexual politics is the use of power by woman to achieve whatever she wants and *freely* chooses.'

Cheri Davis Langdell (1985)

'The Injuries of Age and Time'

For a woman whose plays make what appear to us quite proper claims for the independence of her sex, Aphra Behn numbered among her closest acquaintances many men – apart from the king himself, the likes of Sedley, Buckingham, and Rochester – who were liberated in their own sexuality, but unenlightened in their attitudes towards women. Rochester, like most of these courtly wits, was no 'mere' rake; and is even credited with training one of his mistresses, Elizabeth Barry, for the stage: characteristically, however, he undertook the exercise not so much from interest in her own non-sexual attributes, but for a wager with his male companions. Aphra Behn was not only indebted to Rochester as a patron, but also appears genuinely to have liked and admired the man, with whom she exchanged bawdy poems. A chronic drunkard as well as a poet, a ravisher of pretty women and a fancier of young boys, Rochester, who was generally considered the model for the fashionable wit Dorimant in Etherege's *The Man of Mode,* was capable of scandalising even the king's sense of decency with some of his more public outrages.

Rochester may well have been on Mrs. Behn's mind when she tried to make Willmore in *The Rover* so sexually magnetic. But there were others in Aphra's circle with a claim to be the model for such a character. There was John Greenhill, the highly talented portrait painter, who, like Rochester, died of his excesses in his early thirties. Aphra Behn wrote an elegy to his memory and sent a copy to Rochester: he had, at least been spared 'the injuries of age and time'. In lighter-hearted vein, she made poetic mock of another male acquaintance for his misfortune in contracting syphilis – not an uncommon ailment in her circle, and one from which Mrs. Behn was possibly herself a sufferer in later years. If so, she probably picked up the disease during the longest and stormiest of her own love affairs, with the bisexual rake, lawyer, man of letters, and chief claimant to be the original of Willmore – John Hoyle.

Suspected of the republican sympathies which had led his father to take his own life, Hoyle was in other respects entirely a man of the Restoration. He was attractive to women, and appears to have treated all his conquests with the amused contempt which so exasperated Aphra Behn. Her poems suggest that, despite her own previous liaisons, this affair – which would have been at its tempestuous height around the time she was writing *The Rover* – was the one in which she felt the most complete consummation of her sexual passion. Yet Hoyle kept Aphra, like all his mistresses, at a distance, pursuing his other affairs while wishing Aphra to remain faithful to him alone; inflicting casual insults upon her, yet highly sensitive to any imagined slights in her own behaviour.

Aphra Behn's remaining letters to Hoyle seem to be half-persuading, half-pleading for the kind of freedom, combined with commitment of the heart, to which Hellena in *The Rover* believes she had led Willmore. But Aphra's biographer Angeline Goreau suggests that part of Hoyle's attraction was precisely the knowledge that she would never be called upon to act out the role of wife for him, any more than that of conventional mistress. She suffered, but she kept her freedom. So, presumably, did her Hellena – who fails conspicuously to appear alongside the merry widower Willmore in *The Second Part of The Rover.*

The death of Charles II in 1685 marked the close of an era that had already turned sour. John Hoyle was tried inconclusively for sodomy in 1687, by which time the affair with Aphra was probably over. He outlived her only by three years, before being killed in a tavern brawl – for which his murderer successfully pleaded self-defence. Greenhill and Rochester were already dead, burned out by debauchery, and Buckingham was not only out of favour politically but 'worn to a thread with whoring'. Among Aphra Behn's play-writing friends, Wycherley was in a debtors' prison, Nathaniel Lee was on public exhibition in a madhouse, and Otway was starving to death in a slum – despite, it seems, some financial help from Aphra, personally although she was in debt. She herself died with a fine sense of timing, a few days after the coronation of William and Mary, whose accession ended the Stuart dynasty with whose values Mrs. Behn was so closely identified. *The Rover,* written in 1677, just a year before the 'Popish Plot', may in retrospect be seen as one of the last celebrations of the Restoration spirit, in which no sense of doubt or danger lurks in the darker corners of bedchamber or tavern.

'In the preface to her third play, *The Dutch Lover,* [Aphra Behn] explicitly disclaimed the existence of theme or moral in her writings; nevertheless, broken or loveless marriages and the distress caused by arranged marriages appear in a majority of her works. Like Otway, she was concerned with tracing the effects of broken friendship. . . .'

A.H. Scouten (1976)

'[The Willmore of *The Second Part of The Rover*] is even more Wilmot than in Part One. Hellena, whom he married at the end of the first part, had died, and he is now in Madrid and in pursuit of a famous courtesan, La Nuche, played by Elizabeth Barry. This too couldn't have escaped many in the audience. Rochester's affair with Elizabeth Barry was well known. Here she was in effect playing herself. Appropriately in the end she agrees to go away with Willmore without the benefit of marriage, which he describes as "formal foppery".'

Maureen Duffy (1977)

'The Rover' as Restoration Comedy

The critic of Aphra Behn's plays finds himself (or, more often of late, herself) in a paradoxical position. The works are inseparably linked with those social and political conditions which I have tried to outline in earlier sections, as they are to their author's personal feelings about those conditions. Yet we know so few details of Aphra's life, outside her purely professional activities, that any conjectural reconstruction inevitably leads us . . . back full-circle to the plays themselves.

Perhaps the chief gain from getting caught up in this critical double-bind is the way in which characters in her plays – which one would otherwise tend to categorise as 'types' – come to take on ampler dimensions. There was an influential book of my student years called *The Gay Couple in Restoration Comedy* – which might valuably have explored the homosexual elements its title now seems to suggest, but which in those days was concerned with witty gallants and their pert mistresses. It would thus have 'placed' Willmore and Hellena in a convenient literary lineage which stretched from Beatrice and Benedick to Mirabell and Millamant . . . and extended, for that matter, to Jack Tanner and Ann Whitefield. It suggested, in short, a tradition which has more to do with the 'enduring' psychological interest of love-hate relationships, or the downright metaphysical workings of some Shavian life-force, than with the societies in which such forms of sexual masquerade could be enacted. But Mrs. Behn's 'gay couple' in *The Rover* conduct their duels of wit within a complex web of sexual, social, and economic prejudices inseparable from their time.

Or, to take a different tangent: the character regarded by most critics, even the most sympathetic, as an unsatisfactory loose-end to the plot, Angellica Bianca, becomes, through her acronymic as well as her temperamental similarity to her creator . . . not anything as simple as an authorial mouthpiece, or as theatrically irrelevant as a self-portrait, but a 'loose-end' left over by society itself. Angellica is the sexually-attractive woman who has rejected the loss of independence involved in marriage: she has therefore exploited her only form of inherited 'capital' – her looks – in part as revenge against the male sex, which has reduced her to that expedient. But the repudiation by Willmore represents for her not just the scorning of real love painfully exposed, but a first reminder that loss of beauty will leave her with a future of economic uncertainty as well as personal loneliness.

When L. C. Knights launched his influential attack on Restoration comedy just before the Second World War, he was using the term in its commonly vague sense, to embrace the work of Congreve, Vanbrugh, and even Farquhar – all of whom wrote long after the values of the 'chronological' Restoration had been extinguished, and who were all too conscious of the moral critique of their work initiated in 1698 by Jeremy Collier. A century or so later,

all that an apologetic Charles Lamb could suggest by way of excuse for these dissolute comedies was that they were 'artificial', set in a 'Utopia of gallantry' with 'no reference whatsoever to the world that is'. Whether or not that is true of the later plays of Congreve and Vanbrugh, Aphra Behn helps us to view the actual world of the Restoration from a new angle which also gives appropriate depth to the work of Etherege, Otway, or Wycherley, and confirms that all are writing about a very 'real' if limited range of experience.

The Rover, of course, is unusual in that it is not set in the fashionable West End drawing-rooms and walks of Restoration London, but in a recent past to which a due proportion of its audiences in 1677 probably looked back a mite nostalgically. True, this is still the world of 'the town', and the foolish country gull Ned Blunt can expect to fall into its snares as surely as he would have done in London: but the advantage of 'foreignness' also means that Belvile and his companions are less sure-footed socially, just as they are free of the constraints of class expectations or family ties. And such, as I have suggested earlier, are probably among the underlying causes of the 'actual' Restoration spirit.

And so, perhaps a trifle schematically, Aphra Behn shows her exiles spanning a whole spectrum of attitudes to women and to love – from the mere loutishness of Blunt, through the butterfly charm of Willmore, to the romantic single-heartedness of Belvile. Each has his theatrical ancestors, but each is also part of an historical moment. Each meets his match, and gets his sexual if not his moral desserts.

All moral judgements are relative. When Gilbert Burnet cautioned Rochester against womanising, his ostensibly Christian grounds of reproof were that it was wrong to rob a father or a husband of their property. When Hellena casts off her gypsy disguise and reveals that she has a fortune at her disposal, the *only* choice she has in deciding its and her own fate is between a nunnery and marriage. In declaring for Willmore, she is 'disposing' of her fortune indeed. It *should* not have been so, of course: but precisely because Mrs. Behn's characters are *not* living in Charles Lamb's artificial world, it would have been pointless for her to attempt any more 'morally appropriate' conclusion. The only alternative is the semi-independence enjoyed by Angellica, and Mrs. Behn does not attempt to suggest a conclusion to that.

Many of those parents who preferred to trust their own financial acumen rather than their daughter's emotional inclinations in choosing her a husband sincerely believed that lasting security was more important to a woman than fleeting sexual excitement. Restoration comedy occasionally twisted the rules of the game by allowing the two to coincide – but it also accepted that 'rules' which did not generally relate love to marriage therefore permitted love outside marriage. The alleged hypocrisy of such plays is arguably the reverse – an openness, confessedly uncritical, about a state of sexual affairs which continued well into the Victorian era, although by that time such openness was found offensive.

Our own century's response to Restoration comedy suggests that it continues to touch us near the quick. It was only permissible as a kind of make-believe once the romantics had idealised sexual relationships without altering their economic base; but it came into a somewhat prettified version of its own during the nineteen-twenties, when a fresh wave of the sexual revolution broke – but again touched only the upper classes. Once the bright young things were swept away, it suffered stern critical rebuffs in the self-improving 'forties, until the 'permissive society' seemed to be spreading a gospel of sexual openness to all sections of society. Then came the feminist consciousness that 'openness' no more meant equality in the nineteen-seventies than it had in the sixteen-seventies.

As a feminist in her own time, that is one of the things that Mrs. Behn had been saying all along. As a professional playwright with no alternative source of income, she could not, however, say it very loudly. That was *her* critical double-bind.

For Further Reading

There is no adequate modern edition of Mrs. Behn's complete works. The fullest, but textually unsatisfactory collection is *The Works*, edited in six volumes by Montague Summers (London, 1915), subsequently available in a facsimile reprint (New York: Phaeton Press, 1967). Both parts of *The Rover* are in the first volume. There is a useful but now out-of-print edition of our play edited by Frederick M. Link in the Regents Restoration Drama Series (London: Arnold, 1967), and it was also included in the second volume of *Restoration Comedy*, edited by A.N. Jeffares (London, 1974). Of Aphra Behn's other plays, *The Dutch Lover* is included in a useful one-volume selection of her works, *Selected Writings of the Ingenious Mrs. Aphra Behn*, edited by Robert Phelps (New York: Grove Press, 1950). *The Emperor of the Moon* is in *Ten English Farces*, edited by Leo Hughes and A.H. Scouten (Austin: University of Texas Press, 1948), while *The Lucky Chance* is available both in a separate edition (London: Methuen, 1984) and in an anthology, *The Female Wits*, edited by Fidelis Morgan (London: Virago, 1981), which, besides helpful background material, also assembles work by four of Behn's near-contemporaries – plus the male-chauvinist lampoon against them from which the anthology takes its title. Mrs. Behn's best-known novel, *Oroonoko*, is readily accessible in an Everyman collection *Shorter Novels: Jacobean and Restoration*, edited by Philip Henderson (London: Dent, 1930), and will be published in a single edition by Methuen in October 1986.

Among the biographies of Behn, the earliest modern work, V. Sackville-West's brief *Aphra Behn: the Incomparable Astrea* (London: Gerald Howe, 1927) is now more revealing of its author than its subject. George Woodcock's *The Incomparable Aphra* (London: Boardman, 1948) remains of interest, but Emily Hahn's *Aphra Behn* (London: Cape, 1951) is less substantial than its length might suggest. W.J. Cameron's *New Light on Aphra Behn* (University of Auckland Press, 1961) was important for scholars in restoring limited authority to the anonymous and long-disputed *Life and Memoirs* of 1696, but its findings have been incorporated and supplemented in two more recent biographies, Maureen Duffy's *The Passionate Shepherdess: Aphra Behn* (London: Cape, 1977) and Angeline Goreau's *Reconstructing Aphra* (Oxford University Press, 1980). This latter illuminatingly recreates the socio-political context in which Aphra wrote, while the former is more pertinently critical about the works themselves. Frederick M. Link's *Behn* (New York: Twayne, 1968) is the only full-length critical study, but all three of these last titles include extensive bibliographies.

Despite the recent upsurge of interest in feminist writing, there is suprisingly little, apart from Fidelis Morgan's collection cited above, offering adequate coverage of this aspect of the Restoration period. Exceptions are Rosamond Gilder's *Enter the Actress* (London: Harrap, 1931), a pioneering study far wider in scope than its title suggests; and Nancy Cotton's *Women Playwrights in England, c. 1363-1750* (Lewisburg: Bucknell University Press, 1980). Henry W. Lanier's *The First English Actresses* (New York, 1931), E.J. Gagen's *The New Woman: Her Emergence in English Drama* (New York, 1954), and J.H. Wilson's *All the King's Ladies* (Chicago, 1958) remain of interest, while this last author's *The Court Wits of the Restoration* (Princeton, 1948) provides a broader socio-literary context. Of the many general studies of Restoration theatre, the introduction to the definitive but massive 'calendar', *The London Stage*, has helpfully been reprinted as a separate volume, *The London Stage 1660-1700: a Critical Introduction* by Emmett L. Avery and Arthur H. Scouten (Carbondale: Southern Illinois University Press, 1968), while the fifth volume of *The Revels History of Drama in English*, covering the period 1660 to 1750, edited by John Loftis and others (London: Methuen, 1976), usefully blends theatre history with dramatic criticism. But both volumes are, alas, typical in making only passing mention of Mrs. Behn – and Jocelyn Powell's *Restoration Theatre Practice* (London: Routledge, 1984), in all other respects an extremely valuable work, scarcely mentions our author. The full study of Aphra Behn's plays in their theatrical context remains to be written.

> 'She had been a Tory, a hedonist, a bohemian, and hardly, by the standards of the new generation, a lady. Gracefully, she didn't outlive her own.'
>
> *Robert Phelps (1950)*

Critical Sidelights

'The morality of her plays is *au fond* that of many a comedy of to-day: that the situations and phrasing in which she presents her amorous intrigues and merry cuckoldoms do not conform with modern exposition of these themes we also show yet would not name, is but our surface gloss of verbal reticence; we hint, point, and suggest, where she spoke out broad words, frank and free; the *motif* is one and the same.'

Montague Summers (1915)

'Masterpieces are not single and solitary births; they are the outcome of many years of thinking in common, of thinking by the body of the people, so that the experience of the mass is behind the single voice. Jane Austen should have laid a wreath upon the grave of Fanny Burney, and George Eliot done homage to the robust shade of Eliza Carter. . . . All women together ought to let flowers fall upon the tomb of Aphra Behn . . . for it was she who earned them the right to speak their minds.'

Virginia Woolf (1929)

'Obviously, the best ingredient for guaranteeing the attention of a Restoration audience was sex. Politics was next best, but for a really sure-fire job it had better be sex. A play like *The Dutch Lover* (or any of Aphra's eighteen others) is not much else. Six couples *en mêle* for five acts. All the forumulas and properties in the book are summoned up for duty: the bastard brother who really isn't a bastard; the younger sister who was fatally indiscreet; the maid who drops her mistress's key to the wrong swain; assignations in the woods; the girl disguised as a boy; the long-lost heir; somebody substituted for an expected guest; rakes, bosoms, trysts, masks, swords, honour, the all-important two thousand a year; one grand stew. But Aphra brings it off, neatly, easily, and at the final curtain everyone is happily bedded down.'

Robert Phelps (1950)

'Angellica, who has a complex literary ancestry extending far beyond *Thomaso*, does not quite fit the comic world of the play. She is a woman of the world, and certainly fair game for the Rover; Willmore does not deceive her with promises of marriage, and her experience is more than sufficient for her to recognise that his interest in her is ephemeral and purely sexual. Yet when she is deserted for Hellena, her sense of rejection and her understanding of her situation are so movingly presented as to take her for the moment out of the comic ethos entirely. She reappears, to be sure, as the traditional scorned woman seeking vengeance, but the shift from a believable and individualised woman to an artificial and conventional type is remarkably unconvincing.'

Frederick M. Link (1967)

'Mrs. Behn makes a splendidly representative dramatist for this period. She starts out with old-fashioned romantic tragicomedy, experiments with revenge tragedy, and moves with time into the sex comedy of the 1670s. During the Popish Plot, she turns political with her revision of *The Rump* and anti-Whig city comedy, and in one of her last comedies, *The Widow Ranter* (1969) we find her experimenting with an almost Drydenesque split tragicomedy. She never reached any heights of originality, but she eventually became a highly competent technician, turning out skilful exercises in contemporary drama.'

A.H. Scouten (1976)

'There were other voices who had begun to speak out against marriage-for-money in Aphra's time, but few took the logical conclusion of such a stance as far as she did, nor elaborated it as part of a larger politics of sexuality. Aphra was, though of course she did not know it, at the beginning of a 'sentimental revolution' that would eventually revise England's idea of marriage. Though it was clear Aphra's generation was witnessing a disintegration of the old form, the counsel Francis Osborne gave in his *Advice to a Son* (1656) was still uppermost in men's minds: "He that takes a wife wanting money is a slave to his affections, doing the basest of drudgeries without wages". Charles II confirmed this reality when, in 1664, he wrote to his sister that "a handsome face without money has but few gallants, upon the score of marriage".'

Angeline Goreau (1980)

'The imputation of plagiarism . . . was a minor theme in the diatribe against Aphra. The principal charge was that she had failed in feminine modesty – or as it was more commonly put, that she was a whore. . . . Wycherley nastily comments on her growing "public" fame – punning on the double sense of the word as it was applied to feminine sexuality at that time. . . . The logic Wycherley's joke rested on was well known to everyone: it was the old adage that in gaining "fame", a woman lost it.'

Angeline Goreau (1980)

Imogen Stubbs: GAOLER'S DAUGHTER

Hugh Quarshie: ARCITE

The Two Noble Kinsmen

Tony Church: OLD KNO'WELL

Henry Goodman: THOMAS KITELY

Every Man in His Humour

THE ROVER

APHRA BEHN

The Characters

In order of their appearance

BELVILE, a Colonel
FREDERICK, his friend ⎫
BLUNT, a country gull ⎬ four come out of England
WILLMORE, the Rover ⎭
LUCETTA, a whore
SANCHO, her man
FLORINDA
VALERIA ⎬ three sisters
HELLENA
DON PEDRO, their brother
STEPHANO ⎬ his servants
CALLIS
ANGELLICA BIANCA, a famous courtesan
MORETTA, her woman
SEBASTIAN ⎬ her bravos
BISKEY
DON ANTONIO, the viceroy's son
DIEGO/OFFICER, his servant
PHILIPPO, servant to the English

Masquers, Servants, etc.

Scene: a colony of Spain, in Carnival time.

Scene i

A long street.
Enter Blunt and Frederick; Belvile follows, melancholy.

FREDERICK.
Why, what the devil ails the colonel, in a time when all the world is gay to look like mere Lent thus? Hadst thou been here long enough to have been in love, I should have sworn some such judgement had befallen thee.

BELVILE.
No, I have made no new amours since I came home.

FREDERICK.
You have left none behind you in Paris?

BELVILE.
Neither.

FREDERICK.
I cannot divine the cause then, unless the old cause, the want of money.

BLUNT.
And another old cause, the want of a wench.

BELVILE.
You are mistaken, Ned.

BLUNT.
Nay, 'adsheartlikins, then thou'rt past cure.

FREDERICK.
I have found it out: thou hast brought us here to renew thy acquaintance with the lady that cost thee so many sighs at the siege of Pamplona – pox on't, what d'ye call her – Florinda. Ay, Florinda. And will nothing serve thy turn but that damned, virtuous woman, whom on my conscience thou lov'st in spite too, because thou seest little or no possibility of gaining her?

BELVILE.
Thou art mistaken; I have int'rest enough in that lovely virgin's heart to make me proud and vain, were it not abated by the severity of her brother Pedro, who, perceiving my happiness –

FREDERICK.
Has civilly forbid thee the house?

BELVILE.
'Tis so, to make way for a powerful rival, Don Antonio, the Viceroy's son, who has the advantage of me in being a man of fortune, a noble Spaniard, and her brother's friend; which gives him liberty to make his court, whilst I have recourse only to letters and distant looks from her window.

BLUNT.
Heyday! What the devil are we made of that we cannot be thus concerned for a wench?

FREDERICK.
I dare swear I have had a hundred as young, kind and handsome as this Florinda; and dogs eat me if they were not as troublesome to me i'th' morning as they were welcome o'er night.

BLUNT.
And yet I warrant he would not touch another woman if he might have her for nothing.

BELVILE.
That's thy joy, a cheap whore.

BLUNT.
Why, 'adsheartlikins, I love a frank soul. When did you ever hear of an honest woman that took a man's money? But gentlemen, you may be free; you have been kept so poor with Parliaments and Protectors . . . But I thank my stars I had more grace then to forfeit my estate as Fred has, by cavaliering.

Enter Willmore.

WILLMORE.
Ha! Dear Belvile! Noble colonel!

BLUNT.
Willmore! Welcome ashore, my dear rover! What happy wind blew us this good fortune?

WILLMORE.
Let me salute my dear Fred, and then command me. – How is't, honest lad?

FREDERICK.
Faith, sir, the old compliment, infinitely the better to see my dear mad Willmore again. Prithee, why camest thou ashore?

WILLMORE.
My business ashore is only to enjoy myself a little this Carnival.

FREDERICK.
And where's the Prince?

WILLMORE.
He's well, and reigns still lord of the wat'ry element.

A toast.

ALL.
The Prince!

BLUNT.
> The Prince!

BELVILE.
> Pray know our new friend, sir; he's a raw traveller but honest, stout, and one of us. (*Embraces Blunt.*)

WILLMORE.
> That you esteem him gives him an int'rest here.

BLUNT.
> Your servant, sir. I am a country gentleman from Essex.

WILLMORE.
> But well, faith, I'm glad to meet you again in a warm climate, where the kind sun has its godlike power still over the wine and women. Love and mirth are my business here too.

BELVILE.
> Yet thou stink'st of tar and ropes' ends like a dock or pesthouse.

WILLMORE.
> If I mistake not the place, here's an excellent market for chapmen of my humour.

Enter several Men in masking habits, some playing on music, others dancing after; Women dressed like courtesans, with papers pinned on their breasts, and baskets of flowers in their hands.

FREDERICK.
> No friend to love like a long voyage at sea. Now for some plump girl, flat noses for convenience of kissing, with some brave swelled lips, soft and sweet; their very sweat's balsam in the dogs days. (*Woos one of them.*)

WILLMORE.
> Nay, I'm no tame sigher, but a rampant lion of the forest.

BELVILE.
> See, here be those kind merchants of love you look for.

BLUNT.
> 'Adsheartlikins, what have we here?

FREDERICK.
> Now the game begins. How they eye us!

WILLMORE.
> Fine pretty creatures! What's here? 'Roses for every month'? (*Reads the papers.*)

BLUNT.
> Roses for every month? What means that?

BELVILE.
> They are, or would have you think they're courtesans, who here are to be hired by the month.

WILLMORE.
> Kind and obliging to inform us.

BELVILE.
> But whether they be whores that would have us think they are fine ladies, or fine ladies that play now at whores, is hard to fathom. You must need have a care lest ye be gulled.

WILLMORE.
> Pray where do these roses grow? I would fain plant some of 'em in a bed of mine.

WOMAN.
> Beware such roses, sir.

WILLMORE.
> A pox of fear. Death, will you not be kind? Quickly be kind?

The woman puts herself into the hands of a man and exeunt.

WILLMORE.
> Nay, nay, you shall not leave me so.

BELVILE.
> By all means use no violence here in the place that I was bred. I would not have you at your old tricks here in Carnival time.

WILLMORE.
> Death! Just as I was going to be damnably in love, to have her led off!

Enter Masquers dressed all over with horns of several sorts, making grimaces at one another, with papers pinned on their backs.

BLUNT.
> Oh the fantastical rogues, how they're dressed! 'Tis a satire against the whole sex.

WILLMORE.
> Is this a fruit that grows in this warm country?

BELVILE.
> Yes, 'tis pretty to see these fellows swell and stab at the word cuckold, and yet stumble at horns on every threshold.

WILLMORE.
> See what's on their back. (*Reads*) 'Flowers of every night.' Ah, rogue! And more sweet than roses of every month!

The Masquers dance and go out.

BELVILE.

What think you of these grave people? Is a wake in Essex half so mad or extravagant?

BLUNT.

I like their sober grave way; 'tis a kind of legal authorised fornication.

BELVILE.

Where the men are not chid for't, nor the women despised, as amongst your dull English.

WILLMORE.

But have you made no kind acquaintance yet, since you came to town? You do not use to be honest so long, gentlemen.

FREDERICK.

Faith, love has kept us honest: we have been all fir'd with a beauty newly come to town, the famous Angellica Bianca.

WILLMORE.

What, the mistress of the dead Spanish general?

BELVILE.

Yes, she's now the only ador'd beauty of all the youth in this island.

WILLMORE.

Then let's seek her out. What gallant has she?

BELVILE.

None; she's exposed to sale, and four days in the week she's yours for a thousand crowns.

WILLMORE.

Not possible.

FREDERICK.

Let's find some other game. First let's disguise and muzzle ourselves as the rest have done.

WILLMORE.

Why?

BELVILE.

Because whatever extravagances we commit in these faces, our own may not be obliged to answer them.

WILLMORE.

I'll not change my eternal buff.

FREDERICK.

Nay, you must prank yourself up a little like the rest, for 'tis Carnival and 'tis in honour of our colonel who's come home.

They get gear and masks.

Song.

Sancho and Lucetta come forward.

SANCHO.

These be good game.

LUCETTA.

And strangers too; I know it by their gazing. They're English too, and they say that's a sort of goodnatured loving people, that have generally so kind an opinion of themselves that a woman with any wit may flatter 'em into any sort of fool she pleases.

SANCHO.

Have a care, Lucetta, for these be cavaliers. The dogs are so muzzled and tied up at home with constables and Cromwells, that the devil's in them when they get abroad. There's something of the cock and mastiff-dog in them all that will snarl at anything, one another, rather than not be worrying. Have a care lest they thump you.

LUCETTA.

Is the race of cavaliers not yet extinct or quiet after these thirteen years? I pity them.

SANCHO.

Pity them? Hang them. They're as proud of their persecution as the Jews. They may be down, but nothing dejects them.

The English, being dressed, make a toast with huzzaing.

See how they make their dead Charles saint and martyr. The rogues would make a black-red day for him in their calendar.

LUCETTA.

Sure, Sancho, they have no money to be gulled of.

SANCHO.

Nay, doubt not, mark yon bumpkin that roars the loudest. When did I mistake your game? Go to it.

LUCETTA.

Nay, Sancho.

SANCHO.

Go, or I'll beat thee. Yet, mark, You shall promise much, but pay him little.

LUCETTA.

Fie on your jealous humour. If I understand my trade, he's mine. *(Calls)* 'Roses for every month!'

She passes by Blunt and gazes on him. He struts and cocks and gazes likewise.

SANCHO.

(*aside*). Lo, if some little Eve works in our English garden, the rogues neigh after her as if they were in paradise.

BLUNT.

So, she's taken. I have beauties which my glass at home did not discover.

Lucetta goes out, Blunt and Sancho following

BELVILE.

See, Ned Blunt is stolen out after the lure of a damsel.

WILLMORE.

What, is this Essex calf the first of us to raise a she hare?

FREDERICK.

I hope 'tis some common crafty sinner, that will fit him. It may be she'll sell him for Peru: the rogue's sturdy, and would work well in a mine.

WILLMORE.

Prithee what humour is he of, that you wish him so well?

BELVILE.

Why, of an English elder brother's humour.

FREDERICK.

Educated in a nursery, with a maid to tend him till fifteen, and lies with his grandmother till he's of age.

BELVILE.

One that knows no pleasure beyond riding to the next fair, or going up to London with his right worshipful father in Parliament time. Making honourable love to his day mother's laundry maid and getting drunk at a hunting match. A pox upon him . . . he's our banker, and has all our cash about him; and if he fail, we are all broke.

FREDERICK.

Oh, let him alone for that matter; he's of a damned stingy quality that will secure our stock. I know not in what danger it were indeed if the jilt should pretend she's in love with him, for 'tis a kind believing coxcomb; otherwise, if he part with more than a piece of eight, geld him.

WILLMORE.

'Tis a lucky devil to light upon so kind a wench! Oh, for my arms full of white, kind woman.

FREDERICK

Then talk not, but let's seek one. Come, away. And you too, colonel, leave your dumps and be as you were meant to be.

BEVILE.

Haste with you then. I will ere Lent be come.

FREDERICK.

Away. Let's seek one on the Molo.

They go.

Scene ii

A chamber with a chest in it.
Enter Florinda, Valeria and Hellena.

FLORINDA.

What an impertinent thing is a young girl bred in a nunnery! How full of questions! Prithee no more, Hellena; I have told thee more than thou understand already.

HELLENA.

The more's my grief. I would fain know as much as you, which makes me so inquisitive; (*Florinda sighs*) Nor is't enough I know you're a lover, unless you tell me to who 'tis you sigh for.

FLORINDA.

When you're a lover I'll think you fit for a secret of that nature.

HELLENA.

'Tis true, I never was a lover yet, but I begin to have a shrewd guess what 'tis to be so, and fancy it very pretty to sigh, and sing, and blush, and wish, and long and wish to see the man, and when I do, look pale and tremble, just as you did when my brother brought home the fine colonel from England to see you. What do you call him Florinda? Belvile?

FLORINDA.

Fie, Hellena.

HELLENA.

Or is it Don Antonio the Viceroy's son? Or perhaps the rich old Don Vincentio, whom my father designs you for husband? Why do you blush again?

FLORINDA.

With indignation. I shall let my father see I understand better what's due to my beauty, birth, and fortune, and more to my soul.

HELLENA.

Now hang me, if I don't love thee for that dear disobedience. I love mischief strangely, as most of our sex do. But tell me, dear Florinda, don't you love that fine Belvile?

FLORINDA.

    Hellena, a maid designed for a nun ought not to be so curious in a discourse of love.

HELLENA.

    And dost thou think that ever I'll be a nun? Or at least till I'm so old I'm fit for nothing else? Nay, I'm resolved to provide myself this Carnival, if there be e'er a handsome proper fellow of my humour above ground, though I ask first.

FLORINDA.

    Prithee be not so wild.

HELLENA.

    . . . Prithee tell me, what dost thou see about me that is unfit for love? Have I not a world of youth? A humour gay? A beauty passable? A vigour desirable? Well shaped? Clean limbed? Sweet breathed? And sense enough to know how all these ought to be employed to the best advantage? Yes, I do and will.

VALERIA.

    But tell us, Florinda, how you came acquainted with this Belvile, for I perceive you knew him before we came here.

FLORINDA.

    Yes, I knew him in Spain at the siege of Pamplona; he was then a colonel of French horse, who when the town was ransacked, nobly treated my brother Pedro and myself.

HELLENA.

    Was he not born in this place?

FLORINDA.

    Yes, and went hence to make his fortune. He was in England in the wars and was a cavalier with good King Charles. But when the King was headed he turned mercenary and was in France and Spain and Flanders. And now he is come home with's English friends to see the Carnival.

HELLENA.

    And thee, I warrant.

FLORINDA.

    I must own, I have I know not what that pleads kindly for him about my heart.

HELLENA

    (to Valeria). And you, sister mouse, who goes it with thine?

VALERIA.

    It hath a kind of carnival beating. And though I prattle not so much as you, sisters, my mind's as busy as both of you together. When our brother is gone out in's finery, I have a device to unfold. But see, he comes.

Enter Don Pedro, Stephano with a masking habit, and Callis.

PEDRO.

    Good morrow, sister. Pray when saw you your lover Don Vincentio?

FLORINDA.

    I know not, sir. Callis, when was he here? For I consider it so little I know not when it was.

PEDRO.

    I have command from my father here to tell you you ought not to despise a man of so vast a fortune, and such a passion for you. – Stephano, my things. *(Puts on his masking habit.)*

FLORINDA.

    A passion for me? 'Tis more than e'er I saw. I hate Vincentio, sir, and I would not have a man so dear to me as my brother follow the ill customs of our country and make a slave of his sister. Oh, sweet Pedro, my father's will I'm sure you may divert.

PEDRO.

    I know not how dear I am to you, but I wish only to be ranked in your esteem equal with my friend Colonel Belvile. Why do you frown and blush? Is there any guilt belongs to the name of that cavalier?

FLORINDA.

    I'll not deny I value Belvile. When I was exposed to such dangers as the licensed lust of common soldiers threatened then Belvile, for my sake, threw himself into all dangers to save my honour. And will you not allow him my esteem?

PEDRO.

    Yes, pay him what you will in honour, as I do, but you must consider Don Vincentio's fortune, and the jointure he'll make you.

FLORINDA.

    Let him consider my youth, beauty, and fortune, which ought not to be thrown away on his age and jointure.

PEDRO.

    'Tis true, he's not so young and fine a gentleman as that Belvile. But what jewels will that cavalier present you with? Those of his eyes and heart?

HELLENA.

    And are not those better than any Don Vincentio has here in the Indies?

PEDRO.

    Go, Hellena! Up to your devotion! You are not designed for the conversation of lovers.

HELLENA

(*aside*). Nor saints yet a while, I hope. – Is't not enough you make a nun of me, but you must cast my sister away too, exposing her to a worse confinement than a religious life?

PEDRO.

The girl's mad! Is it a confinement to be carried into the country to a rich villa belonging to the family of the Vincentios, and have no other prospect than that pleasing one of seeing all her own that meets her eyes: a fine air, large fields, and gardens where she may walk and gather flowers?

HELLENA.

When, by moonlight? For I am sure she dares not encounter with the heat of the Indies sun; that were a task only for old Vincentio and his Indian breeding, who loves it here in the dog days. And if these be her daily divertissements, what are those of the night? To lie in a wide moth-eaten bedchamber with furniture in fashion in the reign of King Sancho the First.

PEDRO.

Very well.

HELLENA.

Her apartment, new furbished and fitted out for the young wife, he out of freedom makes his dressing room: and being a frugal and a jealous coxcomb, instead of a valet to uncase his feeble carcass, he desires you to do that office.

PEDRO.

Have you done yet?

HELLENA.

That honour being past, the giant stretches itself, sighs a belch or two, stales in your pot, farts loud as a musket, throws himself into bed and expects you in his foul sheets.

PEDRO.

Have you done yet?

HELLENA.

And this man you must kiss and nuzzle through his beard to find his lips. And this you must submit to for threescore years.

PEDRO.

For all your character of Don Vincentio, she is as like to marry him as she was before.

HELLENA.

Marry Don Vincentio! Hang me, such a wedlock would be worse than adultery with another man.

PEDRO.

You have considered, Florinda, that Belvile has no fortune to bring you to; banished his country, despised at home, and pitied abroad?

HELLENA.

What then? Antonio, the Viceroy's son is better than that old Sir Fifty. Don Vincentio! Don Indian! He thinks he's trading to Africa still.

PEDRO.

Callis, take her hence and lock her up all this Carnival, and at Lent, at the end of the week, she shall begin her everlasting penance in a nunnery.

HELLENA

(*aside*). Shall I so? I am like to make a fine nun! I have an excellent humour for a cloister!

PEDRO.

Callis, make it your business to watch this wildcat. Fie, you're a troublesome pair to me. I would ye were both as modest as your sister Valeria is. – But for you, Florinda, I've only tried you all this while and urged my father's will. But mine is that you would love Antonio: he is brave and young, and all that can complete the happiness of a gallant maid. . . . My father's absence will give us opportunity to free you from Vincentio by marrying here, which you must do tomorrow.

FLORINDA.

Tomorrow!

PEDRO.

Tomorrow, before my father returns, or 'twill be too late. 'Tis not only my friendship to Antonio which makes me urge this, but love to thee and hatred to Vincentio; therefore thou shalt stay here in your chamber and resolve upon tomorrow.

FLORINDA.

Sir, I shall strive to do as shall become your sister.

PEDRO.

I'll both believe and trust you. Callis, look to it. Adieu.

Exeunt Pedro and Stephano.

HELLENA.

As becomes his sister! That is to be as resolved your way as he is resolve upon tomorrow.

FLORINDA.

Sir, I shall strive to do as shall become your sister.

his. But hark you, Callis, you will not be so cruel as to lock me up indeed, will you?

CALLIS.
    I must obey the commands I have.

FLORINDA.
    I ne'er till now perceived my ruin near.
    I've no defence against Antonio's love,
    For he has all the advantages of nature,
    Both youth and fortune, and his power i'this place.

VALERIA.
    You have a defence, Florinda.

FLORINDA.
    I've none. I am ruined.

VALERIA.
    Fie, how dull you are. If you will marry Belvile within these two
    days, neither your brother nor your father can compel you to
    another. 'Tis palpable.

CALLIS.
    Nay, she shall not.

FLORINDA.
    But how? I am pent up and have no access to him.

VALERIA.
    You shall have if I may rule you. If you would have man, you
    must win man, and be a little wanton ere ye be won. And
    therefore you must seek him out, and go disguised lest our
    brother spy you.

FLORINDA.
    I dare not.

CALLIS.
    Nor is it fitting –

VALERIA.
    Nay, listen. I have guises in this chest should serve for all of us
    to go together. (To Callis) Yes, and you likewise.

CALLIS.
    Me?

FLORINDA.
    We dare not be so free.

VALERIA.
    Why think you there be Carnivals, but that men, and women
    too, may be as free as they will ere Lent be come? Nay, dally
    not!

CALLIS.
    You may not.

VALERIA.
    (undressing). Hellena, here's stuff for you.

FLORINDA.
    If Belvile sees me in a guise, he'll think me too free.

VALERIA.
    Nay, you must woo him in semblance of your new person, that
    at first he may not know you.

FLORINDA.
    How?

VALERIA.
    Must I expound to you the very pith of Carnival? Why think
    you our brother Pedro has gone thither? To lie with wenches.
    And why in so fantastic and lusty a guise? To maintain his sober
    reputation to the world. Have not I heard thee say women
    should do as men do? Undress you straight!

CALLIS.
    Valeria, nay, they shall not.

HELLENA.
    Sweet Callis, sweet, sweet Callis –

CALLIS.
    What, go in masquerade? 'Twill be a fine farewell to the world,
    I take it, What would you do there?

HELLENA.
    That which all the world does and take all innocent freedoms.
    (Undresses.) We'll all go together.

VALERIA.
    Put off this moping humour with your clothes, Florinda, and
    assume one as gay and as wanton as this gear. Shall Pedro frolic
    and leave us three mewed up?

FLORINDA.
    Nay then, we will, but to spite our brother. Callis, will you give
    us leave to go and try your future too?

CALLIS.
    Faith, I have an itch of going. If I thought your brother might
    not know it, and I might wait on you –

    She and Callis undress.

HELLENA
    (to Callis). Thou shalt attend and watch us.

VALERIA.
    Then put this and this on.

FLORINDA.

What wanton gear is this?

VALERIA.

We shall go as gypsies.

FLORINDA.

I shall be bashful and know not what to say.

VALERIA.

Fie, be that which I know you inly are. If wenches must needs be demure and nice year in and out, 'tis fit they should be free and frolic for one week in the calendar.

CALLIS.

For as 'tis true, all men are stark mad for wenches, so is it true, however custom pretend otherwise, that we wenches be as inly stark as men.

Music without.

VALERIA.

Hark, it begins.

HELLENA.

Now have I rare itch to dance and to lure fellows.

FLORINDA.

Who will like thee well enough to have thee, that sees what a mad wench thou art?

HELLENA.

Like me? I don't intend every he that likes me shall have me, but he that I like. I should have stayed in the nunnery still if I had liked my lady abbess as well as she liked me. No, I came thence not, as my wise brother imagines, to take an eternal farewell of the world, but to love and to be beloved; and I will be beloved, or I'll get one of your men, so I will.

VALERIA.

Am I put into the number of lovers?

HELLENA.

You? Why, sister, I know thou'rt as hot within as any lady in the Indies.

VALERIA.

Then let's vie with one another who shall first win her man.

FLORINDA.

I'll write a note ere we go, and if I chance to see Belvile, although he will not know me, I'll give it him to let him know Florinda favours him. Yea, and I'll give him too all the letters I have writ but dared not send for fear of my brother.

VALERIA.

Haste, haste.

CALLIS.

Hark how gay it sounds.

FLORINDA.

Fie, Valeria, thou look'st too wanton.

VALERIA.

Why so I am, and will be!

HELLENA.

Let's go.

CALLIS.

Now St. Jago, that is patron of Carnival, smile on our devising!

FLORINDA.

Why then, lead on: Though I be shamed or shent
I'll try my fortune too ere it be Lent!

They go forth into the street and flaunt at diverse Masquers, that are all fantastically dressed. They dance and then run out, the Masquers following.

Scene iii

The street.
Enter Willmore, Belvile and Frederick, Florinda, Valeria and Hellena, dressed as gypsies, Callis following.

HELLENA.

(aside). Sister, there's your colonel.

VALERIA.

And with him two proper fellows.

WILLMORE.

Ha, gypsies, on my life!

VALERIA

(aside). To them!

CALLIS

(aside): Nay, have a care. The devil's in those English when they go abroad.

VALERIA.

(aside). Fear me not. Let's tell their fortunes. I'll begin. (*She goes towards them.*)

WILLMORE.

I would they were not masked that a man might pick between them.

FREDERICK.
    Come, will you drink with us?

Valeria coquettes with Frederick.

HELLENA.
    Callis, do you the like.

WILLMORE
    (to Callis). I like you not, you're sluttish.

HELLENA.
    Yonder in buff's a proper fellow. I'll to him, and instead of telling his fortune, try my own. *(She advances on Willmore.)*

WILLMORE,
    Dear, pretty, and I hope, young devil, will you tell an amorous stranger what luck he's like to have?

HELLENA.
    Have a care how you venture with me, sir, lest I pick your pocket, which will more vex your English humour than a Spanish fortune will please you.

WILLMORE.
    How the devil cam'st thou to know my country and humour?

HELLENA.
    The first I guess by a certain forward impudence, which does not displease me at this time; and the loss of your money will vex you because I hope you have but very little to lose.

WILLMORE.
    Egad, child, thou'rt i'th' right. But cannot you divine what other things of more value I have about me that I would more willingly part with?

HELLENA.
    Indeed no, that's the business of a witch, and I am but a gypsy yet. Yet without looking in your hand, I have a parlous guess 'tis some foolish heart you mean, an inconstant English heart, as little worth stealing as your purse.

                                        They withdraw.
Florinda and Belvile come forward, the other pairs retiring.

FLORINDA
    (aside). Alas, Callis, watches me so, I dare not discover myself. Yet I'll assay. *(to Belvile).* Sir, by this line you should be a lover. *(Looking in his hand.)*

BELVILE.
    Come, let me go; I'm weary of this fooling.

FLORINDA.
    I will not sir, till you have confessed whether the passion that you have vowed Florinda be true or false. *(She holds him; he strives to get from her.)*

BELVILE.
    Florinda!

FLORINDA.
    Softly.

BELVILE.
    Thou hast nam'd one will fix me here forever.

FLORINDA.
    She'll be disappointed then, who expects you this night at the garden gate. And if you fail not, as – *(looks on Callis, who observes 'em)* – Let me see the other hand – you will go near to do, she vows to die or make you happy.

BELVILE.
    What canst thou mean?

FLORINDA.
    That which I say. Farewell. *(Offers to go.)*

BELVILE.
    Oh charming sybil, stay; complete that joy which as it is will turn into distraction! Where must I be? At the garden gate? I know it. At night, you say? I'll sooner forfeit heaven than disobey.

Enter Don Pedro and other Masquers, and pass over the stage.

CALLIS.
    Madam, your brother's here.

FLORINDA.
    Take these to instruct you farther. *(Gives him letters.)*

FREDERICK
    (advancing). Have a care, sir, what you promise; this may be a trap to ruin you.

BELVILE.
    Do not disturb my happiness with doubts.

VALERIA
    (to Frederick). I see, sir, you mean to ruin me. And so you shall, if once you catch me.

She runs off, Frederick following; Belvile opens the letter and retires. Hellena comes forward, Willmore following.

CALLIS.
    Lo, all three have got a man already. I'll not dress thus if I go with them again for very shame no fellow takes me also. And yet I see that women may do most of their business on earth

themselves, if they would but leave their spinning and try. Then if I did not fear my master's anger, I might assay and get some lusty fellow if once I sighted one. (*sees Hellena approach.*) O fie, is this she that is to be a nun? (*Withdraws.*)

WILLMORE.

I am come from sea, child, and Venus not being propitious to me in her own element, I have a world of love in store. Would you would be goodnatured and take some on't off my hands.

HELLENA.

Why, I could be inclined that way, but for a foolish vow I am going to make to die a maid.

WILLMORE.

Then thou art damned without redemption, and as I am a good Christian, I ought in charity to divert so wicked a design. Therefore prithee, dear creature, let me know quickly when and where I shall begin to set a helping hand to so good a work.

HELLENA.

If you should prevail with my tender heart, as I begin to fear you will, for you have horrible loving eyes, there will be difficulty in't that you'll hardly undergo for my sake,

WILLMORE.

Faith, child, I have been bred in dangers. Let it be anything but a long siege, and I'll undertake it.

HELLENA.

Can you storm?

WILLMORE.

Oh, most furiously.

HELLENA.

What think you of a nunnery wall? For he that wins me must gain that first.

WILLMORE.

A nun! Oh now I love thee for't! There's no sinner like a young saint. Nay, now there's no denying me; the old law had no curse to a woman like dying a maid: witness Jeptha's daughter.

HELLENA.

A good text this, if well-handled; and I perceive. Father Captain, you would impose no severe penance on her who were inclined to console herself before she took orders.

WILLMORE.

If she be young and handsome –

HELLENA.

Ay, there's it. But if she be not –

WILLMORE.

By this hand, child, I have an implicit faith and dare venture on thee with all faults. 'Tis more meritorious to leave the world when thou hast tasted and proved the pleasure on't. Then 'twill be a virtue in thee, which now will be pure ignorance.

HELLENA.

I perceive, good Father Captain, you design only to make me fit for heaven. Yet when I begin, I fancy I shall love like anything; I never tried yet.

WILLMORE.

Egad, and that's kind! Prithee, dear creature, give me credit for a heart, for faith, I'm a very honest fellow. Oh, I long to come first to the banquet of love! And such a swinging appetite I bring. Oh, I'm impatient. Thy lodging, sweetheart, thy lodging, or I'm a dead man!

HELLENA.

Why must we be either guilty of fornication or murder if we converse with you men? Is there no difference between leave to love me, and leave to lie with me?

WILLMORE.

Faith, child, they were made to go together.

HELLENA.

Nay, canst thou prove that.

WILLMORE.

Try me.

HELLENA.

So I mean to. If thou will come back to this place after dinner.

WILLMORE.

Yea, what then?

HELLENA.

And if you will swear to keep your heart and not bestow it between this and that.

WILLMORE.

By all the little gods of love, I swear; I'll leave it with you.

HELLENA.

Then it is possible that I may see you.

Enter Florinda and Valeria.

FLORINDA.

Away, away! Sister, our brother comes.

VALERIA.

Up with your masks! All's well. Our men are hooked.

HELLENA.
Yea, the field's ours.

VALERIA.
I warrant you, we've thumped them.

They go.
Pedro crosses the stage and looks on Angellica's picture. Enter
Frederick.

FREDERICK.
Thou hadst a great deal of talk with thy little gypsy; couldst thou do no good upon here? For mine was hardhearted.

WILLMORE.
Hang her, she was some damned honest person of quality. I'm sure, she was so very free and witty. If her face be but answerable to her wit and humour. I would be bound to constancy this month to gain here.

BELVILE.
Oh friends, the welcom'st news! The softest letters! Nay, you shall all see them!

WILLMORE.
The reason of this mighty joy?

BELVILE.
'Tis Florinda's hand!
All blessings fall upon the virtuous maid.

FREDERICK.
Nay, no idolatry; a sober sacrifice I'll allow you.

BELVILE.
See how kindly she invites me to deliver her from the threatened violence of her brother. Will you not assist me?

WILLMORE.
I know not what thou mean'st, but I'll make one at any mischief where a woman's concerned. But she'll be grateful to us for the favour, will she not?

BELVILE.
How mean you?

WILLMORE.
How should I mean? Thou know'st there's but one way for a woman to oblige me.

BELVILE.
Do not profane; the maid is nicely virtuous.

WILLMORE.
Why, pox, then she's fit for nothing but a husband. Let her e'en go, colonel.

FREDERICK.
Peace, she's the colonel's mistress, sir.

WILLMORE.
Nay, then –

BELVILE.
Read here this postscript. (*Gives him the letter.*)

WILLMORE
(*reads*). 'At ten at night, at the garden gate, of which, if I cannot get the key, I will contrive a way over the wall. Come attended with a friend or two.' – Kind heart, if we three cannot weave a string to let her down a garden wall, 'twere pity but the hangman wove one for us all.

FREDERICK.
Let her alone for that; your woman's wit, your fair kind woman, will out-trick a broker or a Jew.

WILLMORE.
A pox on't, I cannot get my gypsy out of my head. Pray heaven, if ever I do see her again, she prove damnably ugly, that I may fortify myself against her tongue.

BELVILE.
Have a care of love, for o' my conscience she was not of a quality to give thee any hopes.

WILLMORE.
Pox on 'em, why do they draw a man in then? She has played with my heart so, that 'twill never lie still till I have met with some kind wench that will play the game out with me.

Scene iv
The same.
Enter Blunt.

BLUNT.
Colonel, thy hand. And thine, Fred. I have been an ass, a deluded fool, a very coxcomb from my birth till this hour, and heartily repent my little faith.

BELVILE.
What the devil's the matter with thee, Ned?

BLUNT.
Oh, such a mistress, Fred! Such a girl!

WILLMORE.
Ha! where?

FREDERICK.

Ay, Where?

BLUNT.

So fond, so amorous, so toying, and so fine! And all for sheer love, ye rogue! Oh how she looked and kissed! And soothed my heart from my bosom! I never tasted such a melting snowy girl. Fred, try if she have not left the taste of her balmy kisses upon my lips. (*Kisses him. Belvile laughs.*)

WILLMORE.

Death, man, where is she?

BLUNT.

What a dog was I to stay in dull England so long! How have I laughed at the colonel when he sighed for love! But now the little archer has revenged him! Well, I'm resolved to sell all in Essex and plant here forever.

BELVILE.

What a blessing 'tis, thou hast a mistress thou dar'st boast of; for I know thy humour is rather to have a proclaimed clap than a secret amour.

WILLMORE.

Dost know her name?

BLUNT.

Her name? No, 'adsheartlikins. What care I for names? She's fair, young, brisk and kind, even to ravishment!

WILLMORE.

Didst give her anything?

BLUNT.

Give her? Ha! Ha! Ha! That's a good one! Give her? Why she's a person of quality. 'Adsheartlikins, dost think such creatures are to be bought? Give her, quoth ye? Why, she presented me with this bracelet for the toy of a diamond I used to wear. She expects me again tonight.

WILLMORE.

Egad, that's well; we'll all go.

BLUNT.

Not a soul! No, gentlemen, you are wits; I am a dull country rogue, I.

FREDERICK.

Well, sir, for all your person of quality, I shall be very glad to understand your purse be secure; 'tis our whole estate at present.

BELVILE.

But didst give her a diamond, say you?

FREDERICK.

Pox, 'tis some common whore, upon my life.

BLUNT.

A whore? Yes, with such clothes, and so attended! A whore!

BELVILE.

Why yes, sir, they are all whores, – I know this place – whores in gay clothes and right jewels; whores with great houses richly furnished with velvet beds, store of plate, handsome attendance, and fine coaches; all whores, and errant ones.

WILLMORE.

Pox on't, where do these fine whores live?

BELVILE.

I'll advise thee.

Enter two Bravos, Sebastian and Biskey, and hang up a great picture of Angellica against the balcony.

One lives near by.

FREDERICK.

Angellica Bianca.

BELVILE.

See there the fair sign to the inn where a man may lodge that's fool enough to give her price.

Willmore gazes on the picture.

BLUNT.

What's this? (*Reads*) 'A thousand crowns a month'! 'Adsheartlikins, here's a sum! Sure 'tis a mistake – (*to the Bravos*) Hark you, friend; does she take or give so much by the month?

FREDERICK.

A thousand crowns! Why, 'tis a portion for the Infanta!

WILLMORE.

Hark ye, friends, won't she trust?

SEBASTIAN.

This is a trade, sir, that cannot live by credit.

The bravos stay and watch.

BLUNT.

What impudence is practised in this country! I'm sure we're no chapmen for this commodity.

FREDERICK:

Thou art none. I'm sure, unless thou couldst have her in thy bed at a price of a coach in the street.

WILLMORE.

How wondrous fair she is! A thousand crowns a month? A plague of this poverty, of which I ne'er complain but when it hinders my approach to beauty which virtue ne'er could purchase (*Turns from picture.*)

BLUNT.

Nay, let's be gone to dinner.

WILLMORE.

Let's get a wench first; some dainty plantation sinner.

BELVILE.

Well, after dinner we'll pass the day as you please. But at night ye must all be at my devotion. For then, I mean to meet Florinda at the garden gate and to marry her.

FREDERICK.

We will not fail you.

WILLMORE

(*gazing at Angellica's picture as he goes*). I long to see the shadow of that fair substance.

They go.

Scene v

The same.
The bravos sitting before Angellica's picture.

SEBASTIAN.

'Tis my opinion this bait will catch no fish. I'd be loath my wages should be deducted out of the first fruits of so mad a project.

BISKEY.

Sure, 'tis a dull trade to sit here watching of shadows.

SEBASTIAN.

Yet 'tis better than chewing cane on the plantations.

BISKEY.

Methinks would have got more in a booth with a picture of an elephant for two pence a piece.

SEBASTIAN.

Yea, a pox on this Spanish avarice that knows not how to enjoy their Indies to the right use.

Enter two whores who spit upon Angellica's picture, Angellica and Moretta above.

ANGELLICA.

See with what malice yon women look upon me.

MORETTA.

They are vexed to find the trade so refined here by a stranger.

ANGELLICA.

Biskey! Sebastian!

BISKEY.

She calls.

SEBASTIAN.

Well, let's praise her still. For vain women are ships that sail only with windy flattery.

Angellica and Moretta enter.

ANGELLICA

(*to the bravos*). Prithee, what said all those fellows to thee that have been here today?

SEBASTIAN.

Nay, they were admirers of beauty only, but no purchasers.

BISKEY.

They were merry with your price and picture, laughed at the sum, and so passed off.

ANGELLICA.

No matter, I'm not displeased with their rallying.

SEBASTIAN.

Yet, one I knew through all his disguises to be Don Pedro, nephew to the general, and who was with him in Pamplona.

ANGELLICA.

Don Pedro? My general's nephew? When the old gallant died, he left him a vast sum of money. Don Pedro? It is he who was so in love with me in Spain, and who made the general so jealous.

MORETTA.

If I am not mistaken, he is the likeliest man to pay your price.

ANGELLICA.

Nay, he's of a humour so uneasy and inconstant that the victory over his heart is as soon lost as won . . . But inconstancy's the sin of all mankind, therefore I'm resolved that nothing but more gold shall ever charm my heart.

MORETTA.

I'm glad on't; 'tis only interest that women of our profession ought to consider, though I muse still what has kept you from that general disease of our sex so long; I mean that of being in love.

ANGELLICA.

A kind but sullen star under which I had the happiness to be born. Nay, I've had no time for love. I have been too busy winning admiration. All the world admires her who gives the frequent and mortal wounds in Venus's wars. I thank my star I have longed for no man yet. What need I, since all I see are offered before I ask? I have refused many but never yet desired one.

MORETTA.

Yet, thou hast enjoyed many.

ANGELLICA.

Yea, but they purchased me at a golden rate.

SEBASTIAN.

You are not like to get it here today, madam.

ANGELLICA.

Aha?

BISKEY.

Methinks love thrives more in a nunnery, than in the open street.

SEBASTIAN.

Ay, for there love grows secret mighty. What would those privy sinners give for the crumbs of lovers that sigh and fall from your bed?

ANGELLICA.

Yea, didst observe, Moretta, how the poor girls crowded to the grates when we passed by; their eyes like poniards in envy of my beauty? Yet, 'tis sad to see youth wither so, like roses in their prime of beauty. How they beat themselves against the grates, like old sullen birds put lately into cages.

MORETTA.

Would we were back in Spain again. What needs this trick? You have youth and future to spare, and may look about and choose your men at leisure.

ANGELLICA.

I would not stay one month longer in this town, Moretta, but for the vanity and pleasure to see and be seen. While the old general lived, his jealousy kept me dead to the world, neither seen nor enjoyed. I had been still as chaste as a nunnery prayer, had my mind been as innocent as his bed. I'll seek my pleasure now and leave a name and memory behind me. The novelty and humour of this device will breed discourse. I know there's few are like to give the money; nor want I any neither. Yet I'll have the gusto to see them gaze and sigh and wish for what they may not purchase. And when our nine days' wonder's over, we'll be gone. Nay, I would eat bran ere any he in breeches in this place should come between my sheets.

SEBASTIAN.

Here's Don Pedro again and another too.

MORETTA.

Sure 'tis Antonio, the Viceroy's son.

ANGELLICA.

I'll fetch my lute, for 'tis for one of these that I have spread my nets.

They go in.

Scene vi

Martial music. Enter Don Pedro and Stephano at one door, and Don Antonio and Diego, his page, at another; all in masquerade. They go up to the picture. Bravos above.

ANTONIO.

A thousand crowns! Had not the painter flattered her, I should not think it dear.

PEDRO

(aside to Stephano). Flattered her? By heaven, he cannot. I have seen the original, nor is there one charm here more than adorns her face and eyes; all this soft and sweet, with a certain languishing air that no artist can represent.

ANTONIO.

'Tis an excellent picture; whose hand can it be?

SEBASTIAN

(above). Van Dyke's.

ANTONIO.

'Tis well done.

SEBASTIAN.

He was a great master and a civil pencil.

ANTONIO

(to Diego). What I heard of her beauty before had fired my soul, but this confirmation of it has blown it to a flame.

PEDRO.

Ha!

DIEGO.

Sir, I have known you throw away a thousand crowns on a worse face, and though y'are near your marriage, you may venture a little love here; Florinda will not miss it.

PEDRO

(aside). Ha! Florinda! Sure 'tis Antonio.

ANTONIO.

Florinda! Name not those distant joys, there's not one thought of her will check my passion here. Fetch me a thousand crowns.

Diego goes.

PEDRO

(aside). Florinda scorned! And all my hopes defeated of the possession of Angellica! *(Antonio gazes up.)* I'll give her a thousand crown ere his be fetched.

He sends Stephano off.
Antonio pulls off his vizard and bows and blows kisses. Pedro unseen, looks in's face.

ANTONIO

(to the bravos). Friends, where must I pay my off'ring of love? My thousand crowns I mean.

PEDRO.

That off'ring, sir, I have designed to make
And yours will come too late. Prithee, begone.

ANTONIO

(aside). Who should this rival be?
Sirrah, go hence; I shall grow angry else,
And then thou art not safe.

PEDRO.

My anger may be fatal, sir, as yours,
And he that enters here may prove this truth.

ANTONIO.

I know not who thou art, but I am sure thou'rt worth my killing, for aiming at Angellica.

They draw and fight. Enter Willmore, Blunt and Frederick.

BLUNT.

'Adsheartlikins, here's fine doings.

FREDERICK.

Tilting for the wench, I'm sure.

WILLMORE.

Nay, gad, if swords will win her we have as good as the best of them. Put up, put up, and take another time and place, for this is designed for lovers only.

The English attack and disarm the Spaniards.

PEDRO.

We are prevented.

ANTONIO.   But by whom I know not.

PEDRO.

Durst meet tomorrow morning on the Molo?
For I've a title to a better quarrel,
That of Florinda, in whose credulous heart
Thou'st made an int'rest, and destroyed my hopes.

ANTONIO.

Dare! Yea, for her or for Angellica
I'll meet thee there as early as the day.

PEDRO.

Then let us both come there disguised again,
That whosoever chance to get the better
May escape unknown.

ANTONIO.   'Tis well. It shall be so.

Willmore having gazed all this while on the picture, pulls it down on one side. It hangs askew.

WILLMORE.

This posture's loose and negligent;
The sight on't would beget a warm desire
In souls whom impotence and age had chilled,
This must along with us.

SEBASTIAN.

What means this rudeness, sir?

BISKEY.

Restore the picture.

ANTONIO.

Ha! Rudeness committed to the fair Angellica!

PEDRO.

Restore the picture.

WILLMORE.   Nay, I will not, sir.

ANTONIO.

By heaven, you shall.

WILLMORE.   Nay, show no swords again,
For if you do, I swear by this dear beauty,
I'll show mine too.

PEDRO.   What right can you pretend?

WILLMORE.

That of possession, sir.

BLUNT.   Yea, by King Charles.

SEBASTIAN.
These be the English that are hither come.

BISKEY.
These be the oaken rogues; all rogues and rovers.

PEDRO.
What, will you fight upon as little reason
As you are wont to love?

BLUNT.   Yea, and as hot.
And in good Prince Rupert's vein.

ANTONIO.
What, not content with civil broils at home,
But you must needs abuse us in the Indies?

PEDRO.
Let's teach them, sir, what 'tis to draw a sword
When it is Carnival. Let's join and thwack them.

ANTONIO.
'Tis well; and yet I'll meet with you tomorrow. (*To Willmore*)
Restore the picture, sir, or leave your lives behind.

BLUNT.
Death! You lie.

WILLMORE.   We will do neither.

They fight. Re-enter Angellica and Moretta above. The Spaniards join with Antonio. Willmore, Frederick and Blunt lay on like mad. The Spaniards are beaten off by the English. All go but Willmore.

Hold, I command you, if for me you fight!

WILLMORE.
(*aside*). How heavenly fair she is! Ah, plague of her price!

ANGELLICA.
You sir, in buff, you that appear a soldier, that first began this insolence –

WILLMORE.
'Tis true, I did so. I saw your charming picture and was wounded quite through my soul, and wanting a thousand crowns to procure my remedy, I assayed to lay this little picture to my bosom, which if you cannot allow me, I'll resign.

ANGELLICA.
No, you may keep the trifle.

SEBASTIAN.
No, you shall first ask us leave.

The bravos set upon Willmore and shoot at him. He dodges and disarms them.

MORETTA.
Oh, madam, we're undone. We shall never see good days again till all these fighting rogues are sent to the galleys.

Re-enter Belvile, Blunt, and Frederick.

BLUNT.
'Adsheartlikins, beat me at this sport and I'll ne'er wear sword more.

FREDERICK
(*to Willmore*). You bleed! I hope you are not wounded.

WILLMORE.
Not much. A plague on your dons; if they fight no better they'll ne'er recover Flanders.

BELVILE.
The devil's in thee for a mad fellow; thou art always one at an unlucky adventure. Come, let's be gone whilst we're safe, and remember these are Spaniards, a sort of people that know how to revenge an affront.

WILLMORE.
What the devil was't to them that I shot at the picture?

BLUNT.
'Adsheartlikins, we'll take it home to England; 'tis ours by conquest. Prithee help me up and I'll pull it down.

ANGELLICA
(*to Willmore*).
Stay, sir, and ere you affront me farther let me know how you durst commit this outrage. To you I speak, sir, for you appear a gentleman.

WILLMORE.
To me, madam? – Gentlemen, your servant. (*Belvile stays him.*)

BELVILE.
Is the devil in thee? Dost know the danger of ent'ring the house of an incensed courtesan?

ANGELLICA.
Fear not, sir, all I have to wound with is my eye. (*She goes in.*)

WILLMORE.
Death! Let me go!

FREDERICK.
Yes, to your lodging if you will, but not in here. Damn these gay harlots. Death, man, she'll murder thee!

WILLMORE.
Oh, fear me not. Shall I not venture where a beauty calls?

FREDERICK.
  'Tis loss of time unless you had the thousand crowns to pay.

WILLMORE.
  It may be she may give a favour, at least I shall have the pleasure
  of saluting her when I enter and when I depart.

BELVILE.
  Pox, she'll as soon lie with thee as kiss thee, and sooner stab
  than do either. You shall not go.

  They draw.

FREDERICK.
  Let him, colonel. We'll get as sound a whore for sixpence in the
  galley that's come in.

BLUNT.
  'Adsheartlikins, I believe the gentlewoman means well.

BELVILE.
  Well, take thy fortune, we'll expect you in the next street.
  Farewell, fool, farewell.

WILLMORE.
  'Bye, colonel. (*Goes in.*)

FREDERICK.
  The rogue's stark mad for a wench.

                                                    Exeunt.

Scene vii

A fine chamber.
Enter the bravos, Willmore, Angellica and Moretta.

ANGELLICA.
  Insolent sir, how durst you pull down my picture?

WILLMORE.
  Rather, how durst you set it up to tempt poor am'rous mortals
  with so much excellence, which I find you have but too well
  consulted by the unmerciful price you set upon't? Is all this
  heaven of beauty shown to move despair in those that cannot
  buy?

ANGELLICA.
  I sent for you to ask my pardon, sir, not to aggravate your
  crime. I thought I should have seen you at my feet imploring it.

WILLMORE.
  You are deceived. I came to rail at you, and rail such truths too,
  as shall let you see the vanity of that pride which taught you how
  to set such price on sin.

ANGELLICA.
  Sin?

WILLMORE.
  For such it is for that which is love's due, is meanly bartered
  for.

ANGELLICA.
  Ha! Ha! Ha! Alas, good captain, what pity 'tis your edifying
  doctrine will do no good upon me. Moretta, fetch the
  gentleman a glass, and let him survey himself to see what
  charms he has. – (*Aside, in a soft tone*) And guess my business.

MORETTA.
  He knows himself of old: I believe those breeches and he have
  been acquainted ever since he was beaten at the battle of
  Worcester.

ANGELLICA.
  Nay, do not abuse the poor creature.

MORETTA.
  Good weatherbeaten corporal, will you march off? The price is
  too high i'th' mouth for you, therefore troop, I say.

WILLMORE.
  Here, good forewoman of the shop, serve me and I'll be gone.

MORETTA.
  Keep it to pay your laundress; your linen stinks of the gun
  room. Here's no selling by retail.

WILLMORE.
  Thou hast in thy time sold plenty of thy stale ware at a cheap
  rate.

MORETTA.
  Ay, the more silly kind heart I. You know the price.

WILLMORE.
  Nay, let me have a pistole's worth of this vain gay thing, and I'll
  trouble you no more.

MORETTA.
  Abominable fellow, I tell thee we only sell by the whole piece.

WILLMORE.
  'Tis very hard, the whole cargo or nothing. Faith, madam, my
  stock will not reach it. Yet I have countrymen in town,
  merchants of love like me; I'll see if they'll put in for a share. I
  am studying, madam, how to purchase you, though at present I
  am unprovided of money.

ANGELLICA.
– Poor angry man, how I despise this railing.

WILLMORE.
Yes, I am poor. But I'm a gentleman,
And one that scorns this baseness which you practise.
I would not sell myself to buy your person.
Though I admire you strangely for your beauty,
Yet I condemn your mercenary mind.

ANGELLICA.
Why dost thou say I am mercenary?

MORETTA.
Sirrah, fool, you must be gone?

ANGELLICA.
How dare you take this freedom. Withdraw!

bravos withdraw.

MORETTA.
Sure she's bewitched that lolls thus tambely by
And hears his saucy railings.

ANGELLICA.   Withdraw!

Moretta withdraws.

(*To Willmore*). Suppose I saw you in the street and liked you,
And came and knocked upon your captain's door
And bade you bed me, would I wonder, sir,
If you asked me the price ere I enjoyed you?

WILLMORE.
Why that's well said. And I'd enjoy you now
At your own rate, but cannot. Thou see'st here
The only sum I can command on earth:
I know not where to eat when this is gone.
Yet such a slave I am to love and beauty
This last reserve I'll sacrifice to enjoy you.
Nay, do not frown, I know you're to be bought,
And, as I think, you would be bought by me.
Nay, I will gaze, to let you see my strength.

Holds her, looks on her, and pauses and sighs.

By heav'n, wench, I would not for the world
Thy fame were half so fair as is thy face.

Turns her away from him.

ANGELLICA.
If you have nothing else to say to me –

WILLMORE.
Yes, you shall hear how infamous you are.

ANGELLICA.
Oh fie, you cant; what am I guilty of?
What, wilt thou moralise that hope to buy me?
You men are strangely partial to yourselves.
What crime is mine that you would not now commit?
Who made the laws by which you judge me? Men!
Men who would rove and ramble, but require
That women must be nice.

WILLMORE.   As you are now:
Why are you coy? I know you're to be had.

ANGELLICA.
Nay hold!
And tell me, captain, are not men
As mercenary as I?

WILLMORE.   Not I, I vow.

ANGELLICA.
Nay, when some lady is proposed to you
To be your wife, you do not ask how fair
Or virtuous she is, but what's her fortune:
Which, if but small, you cry 'She will not serve!'
And basely leave her.

WILLMORE.   'Tis a barbarous custom.
I scorn it in our sex as I despise it
In yours.

ANGELLICA.   Well said; why, now you speak more gently.

WILLMORE.
What's that to you? You know why I am come:
It is by cause of an hot inly flame
The which you fanned.

ANGELLICA.   What's that?

WILLMORE.   Why, lady, lust.
Mere lust for Eve's flesh.

ANGELLICA.   What? No more than so?
Sure, here's a goodly way to win a lady!
What is't to me that you are inly hot?
If I had smiled on all that said the like,
My life had been an everlasting love-bed.

WILLMORE.
Mock not my flame because I speak it plainly:
I know it burns as hotly in your heart.
Why set you forth your picture? Sure, 'twas not

For gold alone. Confess, was't not for pleasure?

ANGELLICA.
Yea, 'twas a mirth, no more, to fetch in fellows.
Enough of that.
Hast not enough good nature to forget
My follies past? I blame thee not for thine,
Although I nothing doubt they were as many.

WILLMORE.
What's that to you or I that live i' the instant?
Then take my purse and me.

ANGELLICA.   Nay, not so fast.
Put up thy gold. I would not sell thee kindness
But for the sake of kindness.

WILLMORE (aside).   What's her meaning?

ANGELLICA.
Thou shalt not buy my love.

WILLMORE (going).   Why, then farewell.

ANGELLICA.
Nay, stay a little. Couldst thou give me love?

WILLMORE.
I'faith, like anything.

ANGELLICA.   Confirm that faith,
And I'll –

WILLMORE.   Do what?

ANGELLICA.   – I cannot tell.
Perchance I'd . . . Nay I would not.
Tell me if you like me. Come,
Flatter me a little and 'twill please me.

WILLMORE.
I'm not a flatterer.

ANGELLICA.   Yet I'll not
Forget the merry but the mean effects
Of vanity which set me out for sale,
And as a lover prize my yielding joys.
Couldst not believe I might be wholly thine
Without considering I am mercenary?

WILLMORE.
I cannot tell, I must bethink me first.
(Aside) Ha! Death, methinks I'm going to believe her.
Curse on thy charming tongue! Dost thou return
My feigned contempt with so much subtlety?
Thou'st found the easiest way into my heart,

Although I know that all thou say'st is false.

ANGELLICA.
By all that's good, 'tis real. Now speak I open:
I never loved before though oft a mistress.
Then talk no more of lust, but rather say
If thou canst love me.

WILLMORE.   Nay, let's not debate
The niceness of a word: so fools do use
To linger out their doubtful joy. Let's to it,
And I will say whatever words you will.

ANGELLICA.
I'll not be won as oyster wenches are.
I fear you cannot credit my good faith.

WILLMORE.
Madam, I've been so often gulled and cheated,
That I've no faith left for the cozening sex,
Especially for women of your trade.

ANGELLICA.
'Tis well. This low esteem you have of me
Hath brought my heart to my command again:
For I have pride that yet surmounts my love.

She turns with pride; he holds her.

WILLMORE.
By heaven thou art brave and I admire thee strangely.
Throw off this pride, and show the power of love.
'Tis with those arms I can be only vanquished.

ANGELLICA.
I dare not hear thee talk; thou hast a charm
In every word that draws my heart away.
Thou hast undone me. Why art thou so soft?
Thy looks are brave and rough, and meant for war.
Couldst thou not storm on still? I then perhaps
Would be as free as thou and all as fiery.

WILLMORE
(aside). Death, how she throws her flames about my soul!

ANGELLICA.
What, lingering still? Do I lack charms to please you?
Am I despised because enjoyed by others?
Are you so puritan a cavalier?
What, dost thou fear that I am over-used?
Try me: and you shall find the mine still golden.
Dost fear these lips are staled by ancient kisses,
Or that this body's paths are worn with use?
Nay, you shall find I am as fresh to reap

As any maid that has not found her harvest.

WILLMORE.
Take heed, fair creature, how you raise my hopes,
Which once fulfilled will give me all dominion:
There's not a joy thou hast in thy hot store
I shall not then command.

ANGELLICA.
                              Content, I care not!

WILLMORE.
Then let's begin the account this happy minute!

ANGELLICA.
And will you pay me then the price I ask?

WILLMORE.
Oh! Why dost thou draw me from my holy worship
By showing me thou art not divinity?

ANGELLICA.
Nay, fool, the pay I mean's thy love for mine.
Can you give that?

WILLMORE.   Entirely.

ANGELLICA.   Swear it then.

WILLMORE.
Why, so I do. Then say no more, but in:
Where I'll renew my vows and breathe 'em forth
In such a wise thou shalt not doubt my ardour.

ANGELLICA.
Thou hast a power too strong to be resisted.

                              Exeunt Willmore and Angellica.

MORETTA.
Is all our project fallen to this? To love such a shameroon; a very beggar; nay, a pirate beggar, whose business is to rifle and be gone; a no-purchase, no-pay tatterdemalion, and English picaroon: a rogue that fights for daily drink, and takes a pride in being loyally lousy? Oh, I could curse now, if I durst. This is the fate of most whores.
Trophies, which from believing fops we win,
Are spoils to those who cozen us again.

                              Exit.

Scene viii

The street.
Enter Florinda, Valeria, Hellena; Callis attending.

VALERIA.
I wonder what should make my brother in so ill a humour?

FLORINDA.
I hope he has not found out our ramble this morning.

VALERIA.
No, if he had, we should have been mewed up this afternoon, which I would not for the world should have happened.

CALLIS.
Nay, linger not here again, beseech you. If your brother comes he'll beat me.

VALERIA.
Then wear your mask. Methinks we have learnt this trade of gypsies as readily as if we had been bred upon the road to Loretto.

FLORINDA.
Callis, fear not.

VALERIA.
And yet I did so fumble when I told the stranger his fortune that I was afraid I should have told my own and yours by mistake. But methinks Hellena has been very serious ever since.

HELLENA.
Hey, ho, I'm as sad as a lover's lute.

FLORINDA.
I would give my garters she were in love, to be revenged upon her for abusing me.

VALERIA.
How is't, Hellena?

HELLENA.
Ah, would I had never seen my mad monsieur. And yet, for all your laughing, I am not in love. And yet this small acquaintance, o' my conscience, will never out of my head.

VALERIA.
Ha! ha! ha! I laugh to think how thou art fitted with a lover, a fellow that I warrant loves every new face he sees.

HELLENA.
Hum, he has not kept his word with me here, and may be taken up, elsewhere. That thought is not very pleasant to me. What the deuce should this be now that I feel?

VALERIA.
What is't like?

HELLENA.
Nay, the Lord knows, but if I should be hanged I cannot choose be angry and afraid when I think that mad fellow should be in love with anybody but me. Would I could meet with some true damned gypsy, that I might know my fortune.

VALERIA.
Know it! Why there's nothing so easy. Thou wilt love this wand'ring inconstant till thou find'st thyself hanged about his neck, and then be as mad to get free again.

FLORINDA.
Yes, Valeria, we shall see her bestride his baggage horse and follow him to the campaign.

HELLENA.
So, so, now you are both provided for there's no care taken of poor me.

VALERIA.
How? I provided for?

HELLENA.
Thou did'st so flaunt and ogle that I thought you meant to lure all the city to thy bed.

VALERIA.
Nay, my man was coy.

HELLENA.
Well, and if you are not yet a lover, 'tis an art soon learnt – that I find. (*Sighs.*)

FLORINDA.
I wonder how you learnt to love so easily. I had a thousand charms to meet my eyes and ears ere I could yield, and 'twas the knowledge of Belvile's merit took my soul.

HELLENA.
Hang your considering lover! I never thought beyond the fancy that 'twas a very pretty, idle, silly kind of pleasure to pass one's time with. To write little soft nonsensical billets, and with great difficulty and danger receive answers in which I shall have my beauty praised, my wit admired, though little or none, and have the vanity and power to know I am desirable. But now I have the more inclination that way, because I am to be a nun, and so shall not be suspected to have any such earthly thoughts about me, but when I walk thus – and sigh thus – they'll think my mind's upon my nunnery and cry, 'How happy 'tis she's so resolved.' But not a word of man.

FLORINDA.
What a mad creature's this!

VALERIA.
See, here come our lovers back.

HELLENA.
But where's my inconstant? Let's step aside, and we may learn something.

VALERIA
(*aside*). I'll draw Callis off that we may be the freer.

> *They go aside. Valeria persuades Callis to go.*

Scene ix

The same.
Enter Belvile, Frederick and Blunt.

BELVILE.
What means this! The picture's taken in.

BLUNT.
It may be the wench is good natured, and will be kind gratis. Your friend's a proper handsome fellow.

BELVILE.
I rather think she has cut his throat and is fled. I am mad he should throw himself into dangers. Let's call and ask for him.

HELLENA.
My heart goes a-pit, a-pat, for fear 'tis my man they talk of.

All cry Willmore. Enter Biskey and Moretta above.

BISKEY.
What would you have?

BELVILE.
Tell the stranger that entered here about two hours ago that his friends stay here for him.

MORETTA.
A curse upon him from Moretta. Would he were at the devil! But he's coming to you.

She goes. Enter Willmore below.

HELLENA.
Ay, ay 'tis he. Oh, how this vexes me!

BELVILE.
And how and how, dear lad, has fortune smiled? Are we to raise up altars to her, hah?

WILLMORE.

Does not my fortune sit triumphant on my brow? Dost not see the little wanton god there all gay and smiling? Have I not an air about my face and eyes that distinguish me from the crowd of common lovers. Oh, such a bona roba! To sleep in her arms is lying in fresco, all perfumed air about me.

HELLENA.

(aside). Here's fine encouragement for me to fool on!

WILLMORE.

Hark'ee, where didst thou purchase that rich Canary we drank today? The juice was divine.

BELVILE.

Well, sir, let's go take a bottle and hear the story of your success.

FREDERICK.

Would not French wine do better?

WILLMORE.

Damn the hungry balderdash! Cheerful sack has a generous virtue in't, inspiring a successful confidence, gives eloquence to the tongue and vigour to the soul, and has in a few hours completed all my hopes and wishes! There's nothing left to raise a new desire in me. Come, let's be gay and wanton. Here are friends that will supply us. *(Jingles gold.)* Hark what a charming sound they make.

BLUNT.

But hark'ee, sir, you are not married, are you?

WILLMORE.

All the honey of matrimony but none of the sting, friend.

BLUNT.

'Adsheartlikins, thou'rt a fortunate rogue. Well, here's two of us provided for!

FREDERICK.

By this light, y'are happy men.

BLUNT.

Fortune is pleased to smile on us, gentlemen, to smile on us.

Enter Sancho and pulls down Blunt by the sleeve; the cavaliers go aside.

SANCHO.

Sir, my lady expects you. She has removed all that might oppose your will and pleasure, and is impatient till you come.

BLUNT.

'Adsheartlikins, her husband is gone hence. Sir, I'll attend you

– Oh the happiest rogue! I'll take no leave, lest they either dog me or stay me.

Exit with Sancho.

FREDERICK.

Lo, how Ned's in a lure. I hope she'll dress him for our mirth, cheat him of all, then have him well-favouredly banged, and turned out at midnight.

BELVILE.

So, captain, the little gypsy is forgot?

WILLMORE.

A mischief on thee for putting her into my thoughts! I had quite forgot her else, and this night's debauch had drunk her quite down.

Florinda, Valeria and Hellena approach.

HELLENA.

Had it so, good captain!

WILLMORE

(aside). Ha! I hope she did not hear me!

HELLENA.

What, afraid of such a champion?

WILLMORE.

Oh, you're a fine lady of your word, are you not? To make a man languish a whole day –

HELLENA.

In tedious search of me.

WILLMORE.

Egad, child, thou'rt in the right. Hadst thou seen what a melancholy dog I have been since I was a lover, how I walked the streets like a Capuchin, with my hands in my sleeves – faith sweetheart, thou wouldst pity me.

HELLENA.

(aside). Now if I should be hanged I can't be angry with him, he dissembles so heartily – Alas, good captain, what pains you have taken; now were I ungrateful not to reward so true a servant.

WILLMORE.

Poor soul, that's kindly said; I see thou barest a conscience. Come then, for a beginning, show me thy dear face.

HELLENA.

I'm afraid, my small acquaintance, you have been staying that swingeing stomach you boasted of this morning. I then remember my little collation would have gone down with you without the sauce of a handsome face. Is your stomach so queasy now?

WILLMORE.

Faith, long fasting, child, spoils a man's appetite. Yet if you durst treat, I could so lay about me still –

HELLENA.

And would you fall to before a priest says grace?

WILLMORE.

Oh fie, fie, what an old out-of-fashioned thing hast thou named? Thou couldst not dash me more out of countenance shouldst thou show me an ugly face.

Whilst he is seemingly courting Hellena, enter Angellica, Moretta, Biskey, and Sebastian all in masquerade. Angellica sees Willmore and stares.

ANGELLICA.

Heavens, 'tis he! And passionately fond to see another woman!

MORETTA.

What could you less expect from such a swaggerer?

ANGELLICA.

Expect? As much as I paid him; a heart entire.

HELLENA.

You see, captain, how willing I am to be friends with you, til ltime and ill luck make us lovers; and ask you the question first rather than put your modesty to the blush by asking me. For alas, I know you captains are such strict men, and such severe observers of your vows to chastity, that 'twill be hard to prevail with your tender conscience to marry a young willing maid.

WILLMORE.

Do not abuse me, for fear I should take thee at thy word and marry thee indeed, which I'm sure will be revenge sufficient.

HELLENA.

O' my conscience, that will be our destiny because we are both of one humour. I am as inconstant as you. For I have considered, captain, that a handsome woman has a great deal to do whilst her face is good, for then is our harvest-time to gather friends. And should I in these days of my youth catch a fit or foolish constancy, I were undone; 'tis loitering by daylight in our great journey. Therefore, I declare I'll allow but one year for love, one year for indifference, and one year for hate, and then go hang yourself, for I profess myself the gay, the kind, and the inconstant. The devil's in't if this won't please you!

WILLMORE.

Oh, most damnably. I have a heart with a hole quite through it

too; no prison mine, to keep a mistress in.

HELLENA.

Well, I see our business as well as humours are alike, yours to cozen as many maids as will trust you, and I as many men as I have faith. See if I have not as desperate a lying look as you can have for the heart of you. *(Pulls off her vizard; he starts.)* How do you like it, captain?

WILLMORE.

Like it! By heaven, I never saw so much beauty! Oh, the charms of those sprightly black eyes! That strangely fair face, full of smiles and dimples! Those soft round melting cherry lips and small even white teeth! Not to be expressed, but silently adored! *(She replaces her mask.)* Oh, one look more, and strike me dumb.

He seems to court her to pull off her vizard. She refuses.

ANGELLICA.

I can endure no more.

SEBASTIAN.

It is not fit to interrupt him, for if you do, your jealousy will so destroy your reason you will undo yourself.

ANGELLICA.

Therefore I'll retire, and you, Sebastian, follow that woman and learn who 'tis.

Exit into above.

This while Florinda is talking to Belvile, who stands sullenly; Frederick courting Valeria.

VALERIA.

(to Belvile). Prithee, dear stranger, though you have not yet lost your love Florinda, you see my friend frankly offers you hers to play with in the meantime.

BELVILE.

Faith, madam, I am sorry I can't play at her game.

FREDERICK

(to Valeria). Pray leave your intercession and mind your own affair. They'll better agree apart. He's a modest sigher in company, but alone no woman 'scapes him.

FLORINDA

(aside). Sure he does but rally. Yet, if it should be true, I'll tempt him farther. *(To Belvile)* Believe me, noble stranger, I'm no common mistress. And for a little proof on't, wear this jewel. Nay, take it, sir.

BELVILE.

Madam, why am I chose out of all mankind to be the object of your bounty?

VALERIA.

There's another civil question asked.

FREDERICK

(aside). Pox of's modesty; it spoils his own markets and hinders mine.

FLORINDA.

Sir, from my window I have often seen you, and women of my quality have so few opportunities for love that we ought to lose none.

FREDERICK

(to Valeria). Here's a woman! When shall I be blest with so much kindness from your fair mouth?

VALERIA.

When my sister thrives.

FREDERICK.

Take the jewel, fool!

BELVILE.

You tempt me strangely, madam, every way –

FLORINDA

(aside). So, if I find him false, my whole repose is gone.

BELVILE.

And but for a vow I've made to a very fair lady, this goodness had subdued me.

FREDERICK

(aside to Belvile). Pox on't, be kind, in pity to me be kind. For I am to thrive but as you treat her friend.

They retire.

HELLENA.

Tell me what you did in yonder house.

WILLMORE.

Yonder house? Oh, I went to . . . why, there's a friend of mine lives there.

HELLENA.

What, a she or a he friend?

WILLMORE.

A man, upon honour, a man.

HELLENA.

I see thy fortune sits triumphant on thy brow. Methinks I see the little wanton god all gay and smiling. Was it your man friend that put it there?

WILLMORE.

So –

HELLENA.

'Ah, such a bona roba! To be in her arms is lying in fresco, all perfumed air about me.' Was this your man friend too?

WILLMORE.

So –

HELLENA.

That gave you the he and the she gold, that begets young pleasures?

WILLMORE.

Well, well, madam, then you can see there are ladies in the world that will not be cruel. There are, madam, there are.

HELLENA.

And there be men, too, as fine, wild, inconstant, fellows as yourself. There be, captain, there be. Therefore, I'm resolved –

WILLMORE.

Oh!

HELLENA.

To see your face no more –

WILLMORE.

Oh!

HELLENA.

Till tomorrow.

WILLMORE.

Egad, you frighted me.

HELLENA.

Nor then neither, unless you'll swear never to see that lady more.

WILLMORE.

See her! Why, never to think of womankind again.

HELLENA.

Kneel, and swear.

He kneels, she gives him her hand.

WILLMORE.

I do, never to think, to see, to love, nor lie, with any but thyself.

HELLENA.

Kiss the book.

WILLMORE.

Oh, most religiously. (*Kisses her hand.*)

HELLENA

(*aside*). Now what a wicked creature am I, to damn a proper fellow.

VALERIA

(*to Florinda*). We must stay no longer. 'Tis e'en dark. Come, sisters. (*They go.*)

WILLMORE.

(*to Hellena*). 'Twill be an age till tomorrow, and till then I will most impatiently expect you. Adieu, my dear pretty angel.

FLORINDA

(*to Belvile*). I'll leave this with you, sir, that when I'm gone you may repent the opportunity you have lost by your modesty.

Gives him the jewel, which is her picture, and exit.
He gazes after her. Exeunt all the women.

BELVILE.

Ha! Florinda's picture! 'Twas she herself. What a dull dog was I!

FREDERICK.

This comes of your modesty. A pox o' your vow.

BELVILE.

Willmore, the blessed'st opportunity lost! Florinda, friends, Florinda!

WILLMORE.

Ah, rogue! Such black eyes! Such a face! Such a mouth! Such teeth! And so much wit!

BELVILE.

All, all, and a thousand charms besides.

WILLMORE.

Why, dost thou know her?

BELVILE.

Know her! Ay, ay, and a pox take me with all my heart for being so modest.

WILLMORE.

But hark'ee, friend of mine, are you my rival?

BELVILE.

I understand thee not. I'm mad! See here – (*Shows the picture.*)

WILLMORE.

Ha! Whose picture's this? 'Tis a fine wench!

FREDERICK.

The colonel's mistress, sir.

WILLMORE.

Oh, oh, here. (*Gives the picture back.*) I thought't had been another prize. Come, come, another bottle will set thee right again.

BELVILE.

I am confident to try, and by that time 'twill be late enough for our design in Florinda's garden.

WILLMORE.

Agreed.
Love does all day the soul's great empire keep,
But wine at night lulls the soft god asleep.

Exeunt.

Scene x

A chamber.
Enter Lucetta, finely dressed, and Sancho.

SANCHO.

Now you look finely.

LUCETTA.

I would I were in truth as fine as now I seem to be. Pray Sancho, let me bear myself gently with my Englishman a little ere we flea him. Go I not gorgeous thus?

SANCHO.

Fie, how thou dream'st, Lucetta. S'blood, she thinks she's Angellica or the Infanta. Are not thy shoulders as laced as mine with galley lashes? Wear not thy dress so low lest he spy them.

LUCETTA.

Nay, 'tis good to go thus when 'tis Carnival.

SANCHO.

Well, thou shalt bear yourself gently enough to make him hot, but not so hot that he undo you. I'll thump you if you lick him.

LUCETTA.

Nay, fear me not.

SANCHO.

He comes.

Enter Blunt.

BLUNT.

Lady, I must beg your pardon for coming this late. There was an accident stayed me beyond my expectation.

LUCETTA

(*Very demure*). Sir, you are not only master of thy own, but of my time as well. I dare not say how much your absence has afflicted me, but rather what joy your presence brings these eyes that love and adore her friend.

BLUNT

(aside). Pox on't, that I had but some fine things to say to her, such as lovers use. 'Adsheartlikins, sweet soul, I am not used to compliment, but I'm an honest gentleman, and thy humble servant. (*Aside*) I was a fool not to learn of Fred a little by heart before I came.

LUCETTA.

You are sad, sir. All's well. My old jealous husband is gone hence, so fear you not but come a little nearer. Your eyes are blue – do you love me? Nay, but be tender. For I am so delicate a lady that I am ashamed to tell how my hear aches for you.

BLUNT.

Gentle soul, why dost thou blush and hide thy head? I never had but one heart, a plain one and as honest, and that's thine.

LUCETTA.

Faith, thy sweet face and shape have made me your absolute captive.

BLUNT

(aside). Kind heart, how prettily she talks! Egad, I'll show her husband a Spanish trick. I'll send him out of the world and marry her; she's damnably in love with me, and will ne'er mind settlements, and so there's that saved.

She weeps.

Why dost weep? Come, no tears. You should smile on love. Come, let's retire, 'tis late and love would roost.

LUCETTA.

Will you be gentle?

BLUNT.

Ay, I'll but sip thee as a cat licks cream. Never trust me else. Yet 'adsheartlikins, I ache for thee.

LUCETTA.

Ah, sir, you speak my pains also. And my desires and love exceed your wishes, though I blush to say so.

BLUNT.

'Tis well, we both are hot.

LUCETTA.

Let's to bed and assay who is the hotter.
Well, sir I'll go in and undress me, and be with you instantly.

BLUNT.

Make haste then, for 'adsheartlikins, dear soul, thou canst not guess my longing and my pain.

LUCETTA.

You speak my sense, and I'll make haste to prove it.

She goes. He undresses.

BLUNT.

'Tis a rare girl, and this one night's enjoyment with her will be worth all the days I ever passed in Essex. Sure, her embraces will far excel all the pleasures I have ever tasted; for I ne'er loved, nor was beloved till now. This is Love's holy-day; the rest were working days, in which I but ploughed the sex. Our dull cold kisses were common seed, thoughtless sown and full of weed, not of force to kindle a heart. Here every look or touch inflames or burns my blood. 'Tis pleasure thus to be stung; for though it swells the heart, 'tis with delight, not smart. I'll take her home with me into England.

Re-enter Lucetta, undressed, with a candle.

LUCETTA.

Are you not undressed yet?

BLUNT.

As much as my impatience will permit.

LUCETTA.

Hold, sir, put out the light; it may betray us else.

BLUNT.

Anything; I need no other light but that of thine eyes –
(*Aside*) 'Adsheartlikins, there I think I had it.

Puts out the candle, and takes off the rest of his garments.
He gropes about to find her.

Where are you, sweetest? – Ah the rogue's silent now. A pretty love-trick this – You need not, my dear rogue, you need not! I'm all on fire already; come, come, now call me, in pity.

SANCHO.

Do not carry the jest too far! (*Hits Blunt.*)

BLUNT.

Ha! (*He is thrown down a trap.*)

SANCHO.

Ha! Ha! Ha! He's dispatched finely.

LUCETTA.
Now, sir, had I been coy, we had missed of this booty.

SANCHO.
Nay, when I saw 'twas a substantial fool, I was mollified. But when you seem to dote upon a seranading coxcomb, it makes me rage.

LUCETTA.
You know I was never guilty of that folly, my dear Sancho, but with yourself.

SANCHO.
But come, let's see what we have got by this. A rich coat; sword and hat; these breeches, too, are well lined!

LUCETTA.
See here, a gold watch!

SANCHO.
A purse – Ha! Gold! At least two hundred pistoles!

LUCETTA.
A bunch of diamond rings, and one with the family arms!

SANCHO.
A gold box! (*He throws it to Lucetta.*)

LUCETTA.
With a medal of his king, and his lady mother's picture!

SANCHO.
See, the waistband of his breeches have a mone of gold – old queen Bess's! We have a quarrel to her ever since eighty-eight.

LUCETTA.
See, a bracelet of bowed gold! . . . Yet, for all this, I fear his being a stranger may make a noise and hinder our trade with them hereafter.

SANCHO.
That's our security; he is not only a stranger to us, but to the country too. The common sewer into which he is descended conducts him into another street. He knows neither your name, nor that of the street where your house is; nay, nor the way to his own lodgings.

LUCETTA.
And art thou not an unmerciful rogue, not to afford him one night for all this?

SANCHO.
Blame me now, Lucetta, to keep as much of thee as I can to myself. Come, that thought makes me wanton; let's to bed. I'll lock up these.

This is the fleece which fools do bear,
Designed for witty men to shear.

He goes.

LUCETTA.
This gold will buy us things? Alas, I curse my future that has made me a slave to Sancho, since I was sold. Would I had coin enough to fly to England and try my fortune as the colonel did. But what base means we girls o'the galleys must submit to, ere we can gain our ends. A common whore, oh fie: one that must yield to all beastly embraces, yea, all the nasty devices men's lust can invent; nay, not only obey but blow the fire too, and hazard all diseases when their lust commands. And so sometimes we are enjoyed aforetimes, but never after.

Blunt calls out below.

And yet I cannot but laugh at this English fool. If I cannot rise in this bad world, yet 'tis some recompense to bring such a fellow down. Lo, now is this bull calf as naked as I was once on shipboard, and now I pity him. There's for thee, poor Essex calf. (*She throws her drawers down into the hole where Blunt has fallen. Sancho calls her outside.*)

I come, I come.

She goes. Blunt climbs out of the common sewer, all dirty and beaten, with nothing on but the thing of Lucetta's which she threw down.

BLUNT
(*climbing up*). Betrayed! Dogs! Rogues! Pimps! Help! Help! Oh, Lord, I've got out at last. Oh, coxcomb! To fancy she could be enamoured with my person! Oh dull, silly dog. Oh dull believing English country dog. Alas, I know not where I am now, nor how to get me home.

Music without.

Hark!
These rogues and masquers must not see me thus.
I fear some beastly ballad to my sorrow
Will be devised and sung here on the morrow;
And yet I know there's many here among
Would in my place, have been in likewise stung;
And though you've better arts to hide your follies,
'Adsheartlikins, you're all as errant cullies!

Masquers come in and mock him and pursue him.

INTERVAL

Scene xi

Night. A garden

Enter Florinda in an undress.

FLORINDA.

Now am I in my way to happiness, and now I ache for Belvile. I have got myself free from Callis, my brother thinks not of me, and I have by good fortune got the key of the garden back door and have opened it to prevent my Belvile's knocking. Yet a little noise will now alarm my brother. I am as fearful as a young thief, and as joyful as – Hark! What noise is that? Oh, 'twas the wind that played amongst the boughs. Belvile stays long, me-thinks, it's time. O fie, the wind has ruffled my hair. I'll get a mirror to make it fine again.

She gets one. Enter Willmore, drunk.

WILLMORE.

What the devil is become of these fellows Belvile and Frederick? They promised to stay at the next corner for me. Now, whereabouts am I? A garden! A very convenient place to sleep in. Ha! What has God sent us here? A female! By this light, a woman! I'm a dog if it be not a very wench!

FLORINDA.

He's come! Ha! Who's there?

WILLMORE.

Sweet soul, let me salute thy shoestring.

FLORINDA

(aside). 'Tis not my Belvile – Who are you, and from whence come you?

WILLMORE.

Prithee, prithee, child, not so many hard questions! Let it suffice I am here, child. Come, come kiss me.

FLORINDA.

Good gods! What luck is mine?

WILLMORE.

Only good luck, child, parlous good luck. Come hither. 'Tis a delicate shining wench. By this hand, she's perfumed, and smells like any nosegay. Prithee, dear soul, let's not play the fool and lose time, precious time. For as God shall save me, I'm as honest a fellow as breathes, though I'm a little disguised at present. Come, I say. Why, thou mayst be free with me. I'll be very secret.

FLORINDA.

Heavens! What a filthy beast is this!

WILLMORE.

I am so, and thou ought'st the sooner to lie with me for that reason. For look you, child, there will be no sin in't, because 'twas neither designed nor premeditated; 'tis pure accident on both sides. Come be kind without any more idle prating.

FLORINDA.

Oh, I am ruined! Wicked man, unhand me!

WILLMORE.

Wicked? Egad, child, those eyes of thine gave the first blow, the first provocation. So doth thy habit. What dost thou thus attired at midnight in a garden but to lure men? Come, prithee let's lose no time, I say. This is a fine convenient place.

FLORINDA.

Sir, let me go, I conjure you, or I'll call out.

WILLMORE.

Ay, ay, you were best to call witness to see how wanton you are and how finely you treat me. Do!

FLORINDA.

I'll cry murder, rape, or anything, if you do not instantly let me go!

WILLMORE.

A rape! Come, come, you lie, you baggage, you lie. What! I'll warrant you would fain have the world believe now that you are not so forward as I. No, not you. Why at this time of night was your cobweb door set open, dear spider, but to catch flies?

FLORINDA.

Sir, can you think –

WILLMORE.

That you would do't for nothing? Oh, oh, I find what you would be at. Look here, here's a pistole for you.

FLORINDA.

For heaven's sake, sir, as you're a gentleman –

WILLMORE.

So now, now, she would be wheedling me for more! What, you will not take it then? Come, come, take it or I'll put it up again, for look ye, I never give more. Come, no struggling to be gone. But an y'are good at a dumb wrestle, I'm for ye. *(She struggles with him.)*

Enter Belvile and Frederick.

BELVILE.

A pox of this mad fellow! I'm angry that we've lost him. I durst have sworn he had followed us.

FREDERICK.
But you were so hasty, colonel, to be gone.

FLORINDA.
Help! Help! Murder! Help! Oh, I am ruined!

BELVILE.
Ha! Sure that's Florinda's voice! *(Comes up to them.)*
Villain, let go that lady!

FLORINDA.
Belvile! Heavens! My brother too is coming, and 'twill be
impossible to escape. Belvile, walk under my chamber window,
from whence I'll give you some instructions what to do. This
rude man has undone us.

Exit.

WILLMORE.
Belvile!

Enter Pedro and Stephano with lights.

PEDRO.
I'm betrayed! Run, Stephano, and see if Florinda be safe.

Exit Stephano.

– So, whoe'er they be, all is not well. I'll to Florinda's chamber.

Going out, meets Stephano.

STEPHANO.
You need not, sir, the poor lady's fast asleep, and thinks no
harm. I would not awake her, sir, for fear of frightening her
with your danger.

PEDRO.
Rascals, how came the garden door open?

STEPHANO.
That question comes too late, sir. Some of my fellow servants
masquerading, I'll warrant.

PEDRO.
Masquerading! A lewd custom to debauch our youth! There's
something more in this than I imagine.

Exeunt.

Scene xii

The street.
Enter Belvile in rage, Frederick holding him, Willmore melancholy.

WILLMORE.
Why, how the devil should I know Florinda?

BELVILE.
Ah, plague of your ignorance! If it had not been Florinda, must
you be a beast? A brute? A senseless swine?

WILLMORE.
Well, sir, you see I am endued with patience. I can bear.
Though egad, y'are very free with me, methinks.

BELVILE.
Peace, brute, whilst thou'rt safe.

WILLMORE.
Nay, nay, I'm an unlucky dog, that's certain.

BELVILE.
Ah, curse upon the star that ruled my birth, or whatsoever
other influence that makes me still so wretched.

WILLMORE.
Thou break'st my heart with these complaints. There is no star
in fault, no influence but sack, the cursed sack I drunk.

FREDERICK.
Why, how the devil came you so drunk?

WILLMORE.
Why, how the devil came you so sober?

FREDERICK.
Prithee, dear colonel, forgive him. He's sorry for his fault.

BELVILE.
He's always so after he has done a mischief.

WILLMORE.
By this light, I took her for an errant harlot.

BELVILE.
Damn your debauched opinion! Tell me, sot, hadst thou so
much sense and light about thee to distinguish her woman, and
couldst not see something about her face and person to strike an
awful reverence into thy soul?

WILLMORE.
Faith no, I considered her as mere a woman as I could wish.

BELVILE.
'Sdeath, I have no patience. Draw, or I'll kill you!

WILLMORE.
Let that alone till tomorrow, and if I set not all right again, use
your pleasure.

BELVILE.

Damn it, tomorrow she's Antonio's.
Would I could meet once with my happy rival.
I'll plant myself under Florinda's window
And if I find no comfort there, I'll die.

Exeunt Belvile and Frederick.

Enter Sebastian and Biskey.

WILLMORE.

Why, this is Angellica's house, I promised the kind baggage to
lie with her tonight.

Offers to go in. Enter Antonio.

ANTONIO.

Hast thou received the thousand crowns I sent?

BISKEY.

Yea, 'tis with the old woman within:

SEBASTIAN.

You're welcome, sir.

WILLMORE.

Who the devil have we here?

Enter Moretta above.

MORETTA.

Don Antonio?

ANTONIO.

Yea, and come to claim the prize I paid for.

WILLMORE.

How is this? A picaroon going to board my frigate? – Here's one
chase gun for you!

*Drawing his sword, jostles Antonio, who turns and draws. They
fight.*

MORETTA.

Oh, bless us! The mad fellow's back. We're all undone!

Runs in and shuts door.

SEBASTIAN.

Help! Murder! The mad Englishman has set upon my lord
again. Kill him!

Alarm bell. Belvile and Frederick return at the noise of fighting.

FREDERICK.

Ha! The mad rogue's engaged in some unlucky adventure
again.

BELVILE.

Pox on't.

Antonio falls.

MORETTA.

Ha! Help! Killed!

WILLMORE.

How, killed? Then I'll go home to sleep. *(Puts up and reels out.)*

BELVILE.

Who should it be? Pray heaven the rogue is safe, for all my
quarrel to him.

As Belvile is groping about, enter Diego, Philippo and Soldiers.

ANTONIO.

I'm wounded.

SOLDIER.

Who's there?

DIEGO.

My Lord!

ANTONIO

Thy hand, prithee.

DIEGO.

Secure the murderer.

BELVILE.

Do not mistake my charity for murder. I came to his assistance.

DIEGO.

That shall be tried. How is it, my lord?

ANTONIO.

I'm hurt. This Englishman has set upon me twice. *(To Diego)*
Carry him to my apartment till you have further orders from
me. Look well to the villain there.

Soldiers take out Belvile. Exit Antonio, led.

DIEGO.

St. Jago! Swords drawn in the Carnival time!

He goes.

Scene xiii

A fine room, dark.
Enter Soldiers with Belvile, and throw him down.

BELVILE.

What a cursed chance is this! Has my humanity made me a criminal. When shall I be weary of railing on fortune, who is resolved never to turn with smiles upon me? Two such defeats in one night. I am here a prisoner. But where, heaven knows. Yet this is nothing to the torture my soul bows with when I think of losing my fair, my dear Florinda. Hark, a door opens. A light! Armed, too! Now shall I die like a dog, without defence.

Enter Antonio in undress, with a light, his arm in a scarf, and a sword under his arm. Diego with him.

ANTONIO.

Sir, I come to know what injuries I have done you English, that could provoke you to so mean an action as to attack me basely without allowing time for my defence?

BELVILE.

Sir, for a man in my circumstances to plead innocence would look like fear. But view me well, and you will find no marks of coward on me, nor anything that betrays that brutality you accuse me with.

ANTONIO.

You are not only he who drew on me last night, but yesterday before the same house, that of Angellica. Yet there is something in your face and mien that makes me wish I were mistaken.

BELVILE.

If you will kill me, I cannot fear you'll do it basely.

ANTONIO.

No sir, I'll make you fit for a defence with this.

Gives him the sword.

BELVILE.

This gallantry surprises me, nor know I how to use this present, sir, against a man so brave.

ANTONIO.

You shall not need. For know, I come to snatch you from a danger that is decreed against you by our laws of Carnival: perhaps your life, or long imprisonment. But 'twas with so much courage you offended, I cannot see you punished.

BELVILE.

How shall I pay this generosity?

ANTONIO.

It had been safer to have killed another than have attempted me. 'Tis the Viceroy's son whom you have wounded.

BELVILE.

The Viceroy's son! *(Aside)* Death and confusion! Obliged by him, who would wed Florinda; the man of all the world I would destroy!

ANTONIO.

You seem disordered, sir.

BELVILE.

Yes, trust me, I am, and 'tis with pain that man receives such bounties who wants the power to pay 'em back again.

ANTONIO.

To gallant spirits 'tis indeed uneasy, but you may quickly overpay me, sir.

BELVILE.

Oh, I'm impatient, sir, to be discounting the mighty debt I owe you. Command me quickly.

ANTONIO.

I have a quarrel with a rival, sir, about a woman whom we love.

BELVILE.

(aside). Death. 'Tis Florinda he means!

ANTONIO.

My rival, sir, is one has all the virtues man can boast of – He challenged me yesterday to meet him on the Molo as soon as day appeared.

BELVILE.

(aside). Death, who should this be?

ANTONIO.

But last night's quarrel has made my arm unfit to guide a sword.

BELVILE.

I apprehend you, sir. You'd have me kill the man that lays a claim to the maid you speak of. I'll do't. I'll fly to do't!

ANTONIO.

Sir, do you know her?

BELVILE.

No, sir, but 'tis enough she is admired by you.

ANTONIO.

Sir, I shall rob you of the glory on't, for you must fight under my name and dress.

BELVILE.

That opinion must be strangely obliging that makes you think I can personate the brave Antonio.

ANTONIO.

You say too much to my advantage. Come, sir, the day appears that calls you forth. Put on this habit.

Diego gives Belvile his carnival gear, and exits with Antonio.

BELVILE *(dressing).*

Fantastic fortune, thou deceitful light,
That cheats the wearied traveller by night,
Though on a precipice each step you tread,
I am resolved to follow where you lead.

Exit.

Scene xiv

A street.
Enter Florinda, hooded, with Stephano.

FLORINDA

(aside). I'm dying with my fears. Belvile's not coming to my window last night as I bade him makes me believe that all those fears are true. – Canst thou not tell with whom my brother is to fight?

STEPHANO.

No, madam, they were both in masquerade. I was by when they challenged one another yesterday, and they had decided the quarrel then, but were prevented by some cavaliers, which made 'em put it off till now. But I am sure 'tis about you that your brother fights.

FLORINDA

(aside). Nay, then, 'tis with Belvile, for what other lover have I that dares fight for me except Antonio, and he is too much in favour with my brother ever to fight with him.

STEPHANO.

Your brother's coming. If my master see me, I shall be hanged for being your conductor. I escaped narrowly for the excuse I made for you last night i'th'garden.

FLORINDA.

And I'll reward thee.

Exit Stephano.

Enter Don Pedro in his masking habit.

PEDRO.

Antonio's late today. The place will fill, and we may be prevented. *(Walks about.)*

FLORINDA

(aside). Antonio? Sure, I heard amiss.

PEDRO.

But who will not excuse a happy lover
When soft fair arms confine the yielding neck?
I fear he's been with fair Angellica.

Enter Belvile dressed in Antonio's clothes.

PEDRO.

Antonio! Good morrow.

FLORDINDA

(aside). 'Tis not Belvile; half my fears are vanished.

BELVILE

(aside). This must be he. – You're early, sir. I do not use to be outdone this way.

PEDRO.

The wretched, sir, are watchful, and 'tis enough you've the advantage of me in Angellica.

BELVILE

(aside). Angellica! Have I mistook my man? Or has Antonio?

PEDRO.

Come, sir, you know our terms.

BELVILE

(aside). By heaven, not I – No talking. I am ready, sir.

Offers to fight, Florinda runs in.

FLORINDA

(to Belvile). Oh, hold! Whoe'er you be. If you strike here, I die!

PEDRO

(unhoods her). Florinda!

BELVILE

(aside). Florinda imploring for my rival!

PEDRO.

Away, this kindness is unseasonable.

Puts her by. They fight. She runs in just as Belvile disarms Pedro.

FLORINDA.

By all you hold most dear, by her you love,
Beseech you, touch him not.

BELVILE.   By her I love?
See, I obey, and at your feet resign
The useless trophy of my victory.

PEDRO.

> Well, Antonio, 'tis well. You've done enough to prove you love Florinda.

BELVILE.

> Love Florinda! Does heaven love adoration, prayer, or penitence? Love her? Here, sir, your sword again.

Snatches up the sword and gives it to him.

> Upon this truth I'll fight my life away.

PEDRO.

> No, you've redeemed my friendship, and my sister.

He pulls off his vizard to show his face, and puts it on again.

BELVILE.

> Don Pedro!

PEDRO.

> Antonio, can you resign your claims to Angellica, and give your heart entirely to Florinda?

BELVILE.

> Entire! This minute let me make her mine:
> I can delay my happiness no longer.

PEDRO.

> This minute let it be: no time so proper.
> This night my father will arrive from Rome
> And possibly may hinder what we purpose.

FLORINDA

> (*aside*). Oh, heavens! This minute? I am quite undone.

PEDRO.

> That we may not be observed, do you walk off to St. Peter's church, where I will meet you and conclude your happiness.

BELVILE.

> I'll meet you there.

PEDRO.

> I'll fetch a father.

FLORINDA.

> Stay, sir, I have not yet prepared my heart
> To entertain so strange a guest.

PEDRO.

> Away; this modesty's assumed too late.

BELVILE.

> Oh heaven, madam, know you what do you do?

FLORINDA.

> Do? Despise the man that lays a tyrant's claim
> To what he ought to conquer by submission.

BELVILE.

> You do not know me. Move this way a little.
> (*To Pedro.*)
> She's coy. 'Tis best I speak to her in private.
> (*Draws her aside.*)

PEDRO.

> I'll be with you straight.

FLORINDA.

> Sir, you may force me even to the altar,
> But you shall never force me to be thine.

BELVILE.

> Oh, do not lose so blest an opportunity!

Pulls off his vizard.

> See, 'tis your Belvile, not Antonio,
> Whom your mistaken scorn and anger ruins.

FLORINDA.

> Belvile!

As they are talking, enter Frederick and Willmore, finely dressed.

FREDERICK.

> Where got you this fine gear?

WILLMORE.

> Why, with Angellica's gold . . . There's my dear Belvile.

Runs and embraces him. Belvile's vizard falls out on's hand.

PEDRO.

> Belvile!

BELVILE.

> Hell and confusion seize thee!

PEDRO.

> I beg your pardon, sir.

Takes Florinda from him.

BELVILE.

> Nay, touch her not. She's mine by conquest, sir.
> I won her by my sword.

WILLMORE.   Faith, didst thou so?

> Then, child, egad, we'll keep her by the sword.

Draws on Pedro and attacks him. Belvile goes between.

BELVILE.
> Stand off!
> Thou'rt so profanely lewd, so curst by heaven,
> All quarrels thou espousest must be fatal.

WILLMORE.
> Nay, an you be so hot, my valour's coy.

Puts up his sword.

BELVILE
> (*to Pedro*). You know I ought to claim a victor's right,
> But you're the brother to divine Florinda;
> I durst not hurt the man she holds so dear.

PEDRO.
> 'Twas by Antonio's, not by Belvile's sword
> This question should have been decided, sir.
> I must confess much to your bravery's due,
> Both now and when I met you last in arms,
> But I am nicely punctual in my word,
> And this mistake another time shall clear.
> (*Aside to Florinda as they are going out.*)
> This was some plot between you and Belvile,
> But I'll prevent you. Sister, come away.

Pedro takes Florinda out.

Belvile looks after her and begins to walk up and down in rage.

WILLMORE.
> Do not be modest now and lose the woman. But if we shall fetch
> her back so –

BELVILE.
> Do not speak to me!

WILLMORE.
> I know I've done some mischief, but I'm so dull a puppy that
> I'm the son of a whore if I know how or where. Prithee inform
> my understanding.

BELVILE.
> Leave me, I say, and leave me instantly!

WILLMORE.
> I will not leave you in this humour, nor till I know my crime.

BELVILE.
> Death, I'll tell you, sir –

Draws and runs at Willmore; who runs out, Belvile after him.
Enter Angellica, Moretta, and Sebastian.

FREDERICK.
> The colonel's mad, I never saw him thus before. I'll after 'em
> lest he do some mischief.

Exit.

ANGELLICA.
> Ha! Sebastian, is that not Willmore? Haste! Haste and bring
> him back.

Exit Sebastian.

Scene xv

The same.

ANGELLICA.
> I am all rage! My first love defeated!
> For such a one who has no other merit
> Than being Don Pedro's sister. Sure he loves her!
> I know 'tis so. He will not see me now.
> He that but yesterday fought for my favours,
> Must now be hired and courted to my arms.

MORETTA.
> Angellica, I told you what would come on't.
> Why did you give him five hundred crowns, but to set himself
> out for other lovers? You should have kept him poor if you had
> meant to have had any good from him.

ANGELLICA.
> Name not such trifles! Had I given him
> All that my youth has ever earned from sin,
> I had not lost a thought nor sigh upon't,
> But I have given him my virgin heart,
> My virgin heart, Moretta! Oh, 'tis gone!

MORETTA.
> Curse on him, here he comes. How fine you have made him,
> too.

Enter Willmore and Sebastian; Angellica turns and walks away.

WILLMORE.
> How now, turned shadow? Fly when I pursue,
> And follow when I fly?
> (*Sings*) 'Stay, gentle shadow of my dove,
> And tell me ere I go,
> Whether the substance may not prove
> A fleeting thing like you.'

As she turns she looks on him.

ANGELLICA.

Well, sir, you may be gay. All happiness, all joys pursue you still. Fortune's your slave, and gives you every hour choice of new hearts and beauties. But know, false man, that you have done me wrong (*Turns away in rage.*)

WILLMORE.

Pox o' this whining. My business is to laugh and love. A pox on't, I hate your sullen lover. A man shall lose as much time to put you in humour now as would serve to gain a new woman.

ANGELLICA.

I scorn to cool that fire I cannot raise,
Or do the drudgery of your virtuous mistress.

WILLMORE.

A virtuous mistress? What the devil should I do with a virtuous woman? A sort of ill-natured creatures that take a pride to torment a lover. Virtue is but an infirmity in woman.

ANGELLICA.

I will not answer for your mistress's virtue,
But I could wish you would persuade my heart
'Twas her two hundred thousand crowns you courted,
Rather than she.

WILLMORE.

Two hundred thousand crowns!
What story's this? What trick? What woman, ha!

ANGELLICA.

Have you forgot the creature you entertained on the Piazza last night?

WILLMORE.

(*aside*). Ha! My gipsy worth two hundred thousand crowns! Oh, how I long to be with her! Pox, I knew she was of quality.

ANGELLICA.

False man! I see my ruin in thy face.
Have you forgot your vows and mine so soon?

WILLMORE.

Faith, no; I was just coming to repeat 'em.
I like you now as well as yesterday.
What though I rove a little now and then?
I doubt not you'll do likewise, and 'tis fit.

ANGELLICA.

I never will.

WILLMORE.

Thou wilt not?

ANGELLICA.

Thou hast changed me. Therefore stay.

WILLMORE

(*aside*). But my gypsy will be here tonight.
Would she would be angry again and leave me.

Enter Hellena, dressed in a new guise.

HELLENA.

Pray, good grave gentlewoman, is not this Angellica?

MORETTA.

My too young sir, it is.

HELLENA.

My mad captain's with her too, for all his swearing. How this inconstant humour makes me love him! Well something I'll do to vex him for this.

MORETTA.

(*To Angellica*). I hope here's one from Don Antonio.

ANGELLICA.

I will not speak with him. Am I in humour to receive Antonio?

WILLMORE.

Not speak with him? Why, I'll be gone, and wait your idler minutes. Can I show less obedience to the thing I love so fondly? (*Offers to go.*)

ANGELLICA.

A fine excuse this! Stay —

WILLMORE.

And hinder your advantage with Antonio?

ANGELLICA

(*to Hellena*). Come hither, boy. – (*To Willmore.*) That I may let you see,
How much above the advantages you name
I prize one minute's joy with him I love.

WILLMORE

(*aside*). Death, how shall I get away? – Madam,
'Tis not convenient I stay with you.
I have a friend – that's dangerously sick.

ANGELLICA.

I see you're impatient. Yet you shall stay.

WILLMORE.

(*aside*). And miss my assignation with my gypsy.

Moretta exits.

HELLENA

(*to Angellica*). Madam,
You'll hardly pardon my intrusion
When you shall know my business. Alas
I am too young to tell my tale with art,
Yet there must be a wondrous store of goodness
Where so much rare and virgin beauty dwells.

ANGELLICA.

A pretty advocate, whoever sent thee.
Prithee proceed.
(*To Willmore, who is stealing off*)
— Nay, sir, you shall not go.

WILLMORE

(*aside*). Then I shall lose my dear gypsy forever.
Pox on't, she stays me out of spite.

HELLENA.

I am related to a lady, madam,
Young, rich, and nobly born, but has the fate
To be in love with a young English gentleman.
Strangely she loves him, at first sight she loved him,
For he, she said, had charms in every word.

WILLMORE

(*aside*). Ha! Egad, I hope this concerns me.

ANGELLICA

(*aside*). 'Tis my false man he means. Would he were gone.
This praise will raise his pride, and ruin me.
(*To Willmore*) Well, since you are so impatient to be gone,
I will release you, sir.

WILLMORE

(*aside*). Nay, then I'm sure 'twas me he spoke of – no, Madam,
I've considered better on't, and will not give you cause of
jealousy.

ANGELLICA.

Well, to your story, boy.

HELLENA.

With this addition to his other beauties,
He won her unresisting tender heart.
Today was the appointed time by both
To consummate their bliss in holy wedlock.
But whilst she languished for th'expected bridegroom,
She heard he's paid his broken vows to you.

WILLMORE

(*aside*). So, this is some new rogue that's in love with me, and
this way lets me know it.

ANGELLICA.

Now I perceive
The cause of thy impatience to be gone,
And all the business of this glorioius dress.

WILLMORE.

Damn the young prater. I know not what he means.

HELLENA.

Beseech you, do not see this stranger more,
For if you do, she vows you are undone.
Though nature never made a man so excellent,
And sure he 'ad been a god, but for his inconstancy.

WILLMORE

(*aside*). Ah, rogue, how finely he's instructed! 'Tis plain, some
new woman that has seen me en passant.

ANGELLICA.

Oh, I shall burst with jealousy! Do you know the man you
speak of?

HELLENA.

Yes, madam, he used to go about in buff.

ANGELLICA

(*To Willmore*). Oh perjured man!
Is't thus you pay my generous passion back?

HELLENA.

Why would you, sir, abuse my lady's faith?

ANGELLICA.

And use me so unhumanely?

HELLENA.

A maid so young, so innocent –

WILLMORE.

Ah, young devil!

ANGELLICA.

Dost thou not know thy life is in my power?

HELLENA.

Or think my lady cannot be revenged?

WILLMORE

(*aside*). So, so, the storm comes finely on.

ANGELLICA.

Now thou art silent. Guilt has struck thee dumb.

She turns away and weeps.

WILLMORE

(*aside to Hellena*). Sweetheart, the lady's name and house –

quickly! I'm impatient to be with her.

HELLENA

(*aside*). So, now is he for another woman.

WILLMORE

(*to Angellica*). The impudent'st young thing in nature.
I cannot persuade him out of his error, madam.

Angellica in rage walks away.

WILLMORE

(*said softly to Hellena*). Her name, her name, dear boy!

HELLENA

Have you forgot it, sir?

WILLMORE

(*aside*). Oh, I perceive he's not to know I am a stranger to his
lady. – Yes, yes, I do know, but I have forgot the –

Angellica turns.

ANGELLICA

Did I not charge you with this mistress, sir?
Which you denied, though I beheld your perjury. (*Walks
away.*)

WILLMORE

(*to Hellena*). So, you have made sweet work here, my little
mischief (*Angellica turns toward the.n.*) – This rogue's bred up to
mischief; art thou so great a fool to credit him?

ANGELLICA

Yes, I do, and you in vain impose upon me. Come hither, boy.
Is not this he you spake of?

HELLENA

I think it is. I cannot swear, but I vow he has just such another
lying lover's look.

Hellena looks in his face. He gazes on her.

WILLMORE

(*aside*). Ha! Do I not know that face? By heaven, my little
gypsy! What a dull dog was I. Had I but looked that way I'd
known her. Are all my hopes of a new woman banished? –
Egad, if I do not fit thee for this, hang me. – (*To Angellica*)
Madam, I have found out the plot.

HELLENA

(*aside*). Oh, lord, what does he say? Am I discovered now?

WILLMORE

Do you see this young spark here?

HELLENA

(*aside*). He'll tell her who I am.

WILLMORE

Who do you think this is?

HELLENA

(*aside*). Ay, ay, he does know me. – Nay, dear captain, I am
undone if you discover me.

WILLMORE

Nay, nay, I'll teach you to spoil sport you will not make. – This
small ambassador comes not from a person of quality, as you
imagine, but from a very errant gypsy. The talking'st,
prating'st, canting'st little animal thou ever saw'st.

ANGELLICA

What news you tell me, that's the thing I mean.

HELLENA

(*aside*). Would I were well off the place! If ever I go a-captain-
hunting again –

WILLMORE

Mean that heiress thing? That gypsy heiress thing? Thou mayst
as well be jealous of thy monkey or a parrot.

HELLENA

(*aside*). Though I'm sure he lies, yet this vexes me.

WILLMORE

You may return, my little brazen head, and tell your lady, that
despite her fortune, till she be handsome enough to be beloved,
or I dull enough to be religious, there will be small hopes of me.

ANGELLICA

Did you not promise, then, to marry her?

WILLMORE

Not I, by heaven.

ANGELLICA

Then vow that you will never marry her.

HELLENA

(*aside*). If he swears that, he'll be revenged on me indeed for all
my rogueries.

WILLMORE

Madam, I swear –

HELLENA

(*aside to him*). Oh, no swearing, dear captain.

WILLMORE

If it were possible I should ever be inclined to marry, it should be some kind young sinner: one that has generosity enough to give a favour handsomely to one that can ask it discreetly, and one that has wit enough to manage an intrigue of love.

ANGELLICA.
By heaven, there's no faith in anything he says.

HELLENA.
No faith at all to thee nor to my lady.

WILLMORE
(*aside*). So now they join to plague me. Would I were out of this.

Enter Sebastian.

SEBASTIAN.
Madam, Don Antonio and Don Pedro sue to see thee.

ANGELLICA.
Come hither.

HELLENA.
(*aside*). Ha! Antonio and my brother. They may be coming hither, and they'll certainly discover me. I'll therefore retire without a ceremony.

Exit Hellena.

ANGELLICA.
I'll see Antonio. Get my coach ready.

SEBASTIAN.
It waits you, madam.

Moretta and Sebastian go.

WILLMORE
(*aside*). This is lucky – Alas, madam, I must be gone and leave you to the enjoyment of my rival?

ANGELLICA.
Dull man, that canst not see how ill, how poor,
That false dissimulation looks. Be gone,
And never let me see thy cozening face again.

WILLMORE.
Farewell, till you're in better humour – (*Aside*) I'm glad of this release. Where is my gypsy?

Exit Willmore.

ANGELLICA.
Oh, with what willing haste he took his leave,
He's gone, and in this ague of my soul
The shivering fit returns.
In vain I have consulted all my charms,
And thought my eyes could kindle lasting fires,

I had forgot my name, my infamy,
And how all men prefer the younger mistress.
Well, sir, since I am not fit to be beloved,
I am resolved to think on some revenge
On him that shamed me thus. Oh Willmore, Willmore!

She goes.

Scene xvi

The street.
Enter the three sisters, dressed as nymphs and with long heads of hair.

FLORINDA.
We're happily escaped, and yet I tremble still. Our brother's angry!

VALERIA.
A lover and fear! Why, I am but half an one yet and I have courage for any attempt.

HELLENA.
But why would you have us in new guises?

VALERIA.
Because our brother hath found out our old ones. And these great periwigs will hide our faces better than any guise we went in yet. Put up your vizards and away.

FLORINDA.
Prithee, what hadst done with Callis?

VALERIA.
When I saw no reason would do good on her, as she was looking for something in the great chest, I toppled her in by the heels, locked her in, and left her bawling for help.

FLORINDA.
'Tis well you resolve to follow my fortunes, for thou darest never appear at home again after such an action.

VALERIA.
That's according as Frederick and I shall agree. But to our business: I delivered your note to Bevile when I got out under pretence of going to mass. I found him at his lodging and never was man in so desperate a condition. I told him of your resolution of making your escape today and to die rather than be Antonio's.

FLORINDA.
Thou should'st have told him I was confined to my chamber upon my brother's suspicion.

VALERIA.

I said all this, and told him your brother was now gone to his devotion, and he resolves to visit every church till he find him, and not only undeceive him in that, but caress him so as shall delay his return home.

FLORINDA.

Swords still? Our devices go awry, and –

VALERIA.

Nay, has not my wit served well till now? Do still as I advise you. How now, Hellena? Silent for this once? Does it go ill with your affairs also?

HELLENA.

I know not yet. Nor know I well how I should handle my mad captain, for he's as hard to catch as a falcon with no tresses.

FLORINDA.

O heavens! Here comes our brother, and Belvile with him too. I muse they are become friends again.

VALERIA.

Up, sisters.

They put up their vizards. Enter Don Pedro and Belvile in serious discourse; Willmore also.

VALERIA.

Walk boldly by them, and I'll follow at distance, lest he suspect you.

WILLMORE.

Ha! Three nymphs! There's one for each of us.

The sisters walk by them, one after another. Valeria looks back on Willmore.

WILLMORE.

Ha! A woman, and of excellent mien!

PEDRO.

She throws a kind look back on you.

WILLMORE.

Death, 'tis a likely wench, and that kind look shall not be cast away. I'll follow her.

BELVILE.

Prithee do not.

WILLMORE.

Do not? By heavens, to the antipodes, with such an invitation.

She goes out, and Willmore follows her.

BELVILE.

'Tis a mad fellow for a wench.

Enter Frederick.

FREDERICK.

Oh, colonel, such news!

BELVILE.

Prithee what?

FREDERICK.

News that will make you laugh in spite of fortune.

BELVILE.

What, Blunt has had some damned trick put upon him? Cheated, banged, or clapped?

FREDERICK.

Cheated, sir, rarely cheated of all but his drawers. The unconscionable whore Lucetta turned him out before consummation, so that, traversing the streets at midnight, the watch found him in fresco and conducted him home. By heaven, 'tis such a sight; and yet I durst as well been hanged as laughed at him or pity him. He beats all that do but ask him a question, and is in such an humour.

PEDRO.

Who is't has met with this ill usage, sir?

BELVILE.

A friend of ours whom you must see for mirth's sake –

PEDRO.

What is he?

BELVILE.

A countryman of ours, one that has been educated at so plentiful a rate he yet ne'er knew the want of money, and 'twill be a great jest to see how simply he'll look without it. Prithee, Fred, do you go home and keep him in that posture till we come.

Frederick goes.

BELVILE.

(*aside*). I'll employ him in this to give Florinda time for an escape. Sir, let us first dally with yond nymphs.

PEDRO.

Content! I'll venture with the second. Do you Belvile, take the third. (*Goes after Florinda.*)

BELVILE.

Fie, what a thing's a Carnival!

Goes towards Hellena and then out.
Florinda advances from farther end of the scene, looking behind her.

FLORINDA.

I am followed too. Ha, my brother advancing this way. Good heavens defend me from being seen by him.

She goes.

Pedro follows her.

PEDRO.

Nay, be not coy. Here's coin for you.

Follows her. Re-enter Valeria, Willmore following.

VALERIA.

Come, captain.

WILLMORE.

Ah! There she sails. She looks back as she were willing to be boarded. I'll warrant her prize.

Valeria goes and he follows.

Enter Hellena, just as he goes out.

HELLENA.

Ha, now my captain has Valeria in chase.
I'll find his haunts and plague him everywhere.
Ha, my brother.

She flies,

Pedro following.

PEDRO.

Do I spy you again? Methought I'd lost you. Stay!

He goes, calling after her.

Re-enter Florinda.

FLORINDA.

What shall I do? I fear my brother still pursues me. Ha! here's a door open. I'll venture in. My life and honour are at stake, and my necessity has no choice.

She goes into the Englishmen's lodgings as Valeria enters.

VALERIA.

This is Belvile's lodging. She's gone in as readily as if she know it. Hah, here's that mad fellow again, and my brother too. I dare not venture in, but will watch my opportunity.

Goes.

Re-enter Willmore and Pedro from different sides.

WILLMORE.

I have lost her hereabouts.

PEDRO.

I've lost mine too. Let's seek out Belvile.

Goes.

Hellena enters aside, watching.

WILLMORE.

Pox on't, she must not escape me so.

Goes out.

HELLENA.

Will you be ever thus? Well, there's no checking him in this humour.

VALERIE.

You must devise some newer trick to plague him.

They go.

Scene xvii

A chamber.
Enter Blunt with a book.

BLUNT.

A pox on this tailor, for not yet bringing home the clothes I bespoke! And a pox of all poor cavaliers! A man can never keep a spare suit for 'em, and I shall have these rogues come in and find me naked. There's the worst of all – the colonel and Willmore, that rogue, will abuse me out of all Christian patience. But I'm resolved to arm myself: the rascals shall not insult over me too much. What a dog was I to believe woman, to be thus soothed into a cozening. (*Puts on an old rusty sword and buff belt.*) A fine ladylike whore to cheat me thus. A pox light on her, I shall never be reconciled to the sex more. What would I give her to have one of 'em within my reach now! Any mortal thing in petticoats, on whom to be revenged. But, here's a cursed book, – that can instruct me how to prevent such mischiefs now 'tis too late. Well, 'tis a rare convenient thing to read a little now and then to ease the mind. O dog. O silly dog!

Sits down and reads. Enter to him Florinda.

FLORINDA.

This house is haunted, sure. 'Tis well furnished, and no living thing inhabits it. Ha! A man! Heavens, how he's attired! I tremble now for fear, and yet I must venture now to speak to him. – Sir.

Blunt starts up and gazes.

BLUNT.

Ha, what's here?

FLORINDA.

If I may interrupt your meditations –

BLUNT.

    Are my wishes granted? And is not that a she creature? 'Adsheartlikins, 'tis – What wretched thing art thou, ha?

FLORINDA.

    A very wretched maid, forced by strange unlucky accident to seek a safety here, and must be ruined if you do not grant it.

BLUNT.

    Why, what the devil, can I not be safe in my house for you, not in my chamber? Nay, not even being naked too cannot secure me? This is an impudence greater than has invaded me yet.

FLORINDA.

    Alas, what mean you, sir? I beseech you, as you seem a gentleman, pity a harmless virgin that takes your house for sanctuary.

BLUNT.

    Talk on, talk on; and weep, too. Do, flatter me out of my senses again. A harmless virgin with a pox; as much one as t'other. 'Adsheartlikins, Dost thou know, miserable woman, into what den of mischiefs thou art fallen? Does not see something in my looks that frights thy guilty soul? Come, no resistance! (*pulls her rudely*) To the bed within!

FLORINDA.

    Dare you be so cruel?

BLUNT.

    Cruel? Yes, I will kiss and beat thee all over, kiss and see thee all over; thou shalt lie with me too. Not that I care for the enjoyment, but to let thee see I will be revenged on one whore for the sins of another I will flatter thee, and beat thee; embrace thee and rob thee, as she did me; fawn on thee, and strip thee stark naked; then hang thee out at my window by the heels, with a paper of scurvy verses fastened to thy breast in praise of damnable women. Come, come, along.

FLORINDA.

    Alas, sir, must I be sacrificed for the crimes of the most infamous of my sex? I never understood the sins you name.

BLUNT.

    A generation of damned hypocrites! To flatter my very clothes from my back! Dissembling witches! Are these the returns you make an honest gentleman that trusts, believes, and loves you? I'll strip you at noonday and turn you out in the street for boys to hoot at. (*Pulls her again. Enter Frederick.*)

FREDERICK.

    Ha, what's here to do?

BLUNT.

    'Adsheartlikins, Fred, I am glad thou art come, to be a witness of my dire revenge.

FREDERICK.

    What's this? Another person of quality, who is upon the ramble to supply the defects of some grave impotent husband?

BLUNT.

    No, this has another pretence, some very unfortunate accident brought her hither to fool's haven. Is the ass to be cajoled again, think ye? No, young one, therefore prepare for both my pleasures of enjoyment and revenge. For I am resolved to make up my loss here on thy body.

FREDERICK.

    Now, mistress, what do you think of this?

FLORINDA.

    I think he will not, dares not be so barbarous.

FREDERICK.

    Have a care, Blunt, she fetched a deep sigh; she is enamoured with thy sword and drawers. I fear she'll strip thee even of that; there are of her calling such unconscionable baggages and such dextrous thieves, they'll flea a man and he shall ne'er miss his skin till he feels the cold. There was a countryman of ours robbed of a row of teeth whilst he was a-sleeeping, which the jilt made him buy again when he waked. You see, lady, how little reason we have to trust you.

BLUNT.

    'Adsheartlikins, why this is most abominable!

FLORINDA.

    By all that's holy, I am none such. I entered here to save a life in danger.

FREDERICK.

    For no goodness, I'll warrant her.

FLORINDA.

    I am a lady of quality.

FREDERICK.

    Very like! Why go you thus tricked out so wantonly?

FLORINDA.

    Why, for 'tis Carnival.

FREDERICK.

    Faith, damsel, we are not fellows to be caught twice in the same trap. Look on that wreck, and see how a female picaroon of this island of rogues has shattered him.

BLUNT.

    'Adsheartlikins, we'll both lie with her, and then let me alone to bang her.

FREDERICK.

I'm ready to serve you in matters of revenge that has a double pleasure in't.

BLUNT.

Well said. – You hear, little one, how you are condemned by public vote to the bed within.

FREDERICK.

There's no resisting your destiny, sweetheart. (*Pulls her.*)

FLORINDA.

Stay, sir, I have seen you with Belvile, an English cavalier. For this sake, use me kindly. You know him, sir.

BLUNT.

Belvile? Why yes, sweeting, we do know Belvile, and wish he were with us now. He's a cormorant at whore and bacon. He'd have a limb or two of thee, my virgin pullet.

FLORINDA.

Sir, if you have any esteem for that Belvile, I conjure you to treat me with more gentleness.

FREDERICK.

Hark'ee, Blunt, I doubt we are mistaken in this matter.

FLORINDA.

Sir, if you find me not worth Belvile's care, use me as you please. And that you may think I merit better treatment than you threaten, pray take this present.

Gives him a ring. He looks on it.

BLUNT.

Hum, a diamond! Why, 'tis a wonderful virtue now that lies in this ring, a mollifying virtue.

FREDERICK.

I begin to suspect something, and 'twould anger us vilely to be trussed up for a rape upon a maid of quality, when we only believe.we ruffle a harlot.

BLUNT.

Thou art a credulous fellow, but 'adsheartlikins, I have no faith yet. Why, my saint prattled as parlously as this does.

FREDERICK.

Yet let this ring reprieve her till we see Belvile.

BLUNT.

That's hard, yet I will grant it.

Enter Philippo.

PHILIPPO.

Oh, sir, the colonel is just come in with Willmore and a Spaniard of quality, and talks of having you to dinner with 'em. But the tailor's not yet come.

BLUNT.

'Adsheartlikins, I'm undone! I would not see 'em for the world. You, sirrah, upon your life, say I am not at home, or that I'm asleep, or – or – anything. Away.

Philippo goes.

Hark'ee, Fred, lock up the wench in your chamber.

FREDERICK.

Fear nothing, madam: whate'er he threatens, you are safe whilst in my hands.

Exeunt Frederick and Florinda.

Scene xviii

The same.
A great knocking as at the chamber door.

(VOICES)

(*call within*). Ned! Ned Blunt! Ned Blunt!

BELVILE

(*within*). Why, he's dead, sir, without dispute dead; he has not been seen today, Willmore. Let's break open the door.

BLUNT.

Ha, break open the door? 'Adsheartlikins, that mad fellow will be as good as his word.

BELVILE

(*within*). Boy, bring something to force the door.

A great noise within, at the door again.

BLUNT.

– Hold, hold! What do you mean, gentleman, what do you mean?

BELVILE

(*within*). Oh, rogue, art alive? Prithee open the door and convince us.

BLUNT.

No, no, no, no, gentlemen. I am at my devotion. 'Adsheartlikins, will you not allow a man time to pray?

BELVILE

(*within*). Turned religious? A greater wonder than the first! Therefore open quickly.

BLUNT.

Why hark'ee, colonel, to tell the truth, I have a wench with me. You apprehend me?

WILLMORE

(*within*). How, a wench? Nay then, we must enter and partake also. Unless it be your lady of quality, and then we'll keep our distance.

BLUNT.

So, the business is out.

WILLMORE

(*within*). Come, come, lend's more hands to the door. Now heave, all together. (*Breaks open the door.*) So, well done, my boys.

Enter Belvile, Willmore, Pedro and Philippo. Blunt looks simply, they all laugh at him; he lays his hand on his sword.

BLUNT.

Hark'ee sirs, laugh out your laugh quickly, d'ye hear, and be gone. I shall spoil your sport else, 'adsheartlikins, sir, I shall. (*Aside*) A plague upon my tailor!

WILLMORE.

'Sdeath, how the whore has dressed him! Faith, sir, I'm sorry.

BLUNT.

Are you so, sir? Keep't to yourself then, sir, I advise you, d'ye hear, for I can as little endure your pity as his mirth.

Lays his hand on's sword.

BELVILE.

Indeed, Willmore, thou art a little too rough with Ned Blunt's mistress. Call a person of quality whore? Ha, he.

BLUNT.

Hark'ee sir, you know me, and know I can be angry. Have a care, for 'adsheartlikins, I can fight, too, I can, sir. Do you mark me? No more.

BELVILE.

Why so peevish, good Ned?

BLUNT.

Look ye settle me a good sober countenance, and that quickly, too, or you shall know Ned Blunt is not –

BELVILE.

Not everybody, we know that.

BLUNT.

Not an ass to be laughed at, sir.

WILLMORE.

Unconscionable sinner! To bring a lover so near his happiness – a vigorous passionate lover – and then not only cheat him of his movables, but his very desires, too.

BELVILE.

Ah, sir, a mistress is a trifle with Blunt; he'll have a dozen the next time he looks abroad. His eyes have charms not to be resisted.

PEDRO.

Sir, though I'm a stranger to you, I am ashamed at the rudeness of my nation; and could you learn who did it, would assist you to make an example of 'em.

BLUNT.

Why ay, there's one speaks sense now, and handsomely. And let me tell you, gentlemen, I should not have showed myself like a jack pudding thus to have made you mirth, but that I have revenge within my power. For know, I have got into my possession a female, who had better have fallen under any curse than the ruin I design her. 'Adsheartlikins, she assaulted me here in my own lodgings, and had doubtless committed a rape upon me, had not this sword defended me.

FREDERICK

(*entering*). I know not that, but o' my conscience thou had ravished her, had she not redeemed herself with a ring. Let's see't, Blunt.

Blunt shows the ring.

BELVILE

(*aside*). Ha! The ring I gave Florinda when we exchanged our vows! – Hark'ee, Blunt – (*Goes to whisper to him.*)

WILLMORE.

No whispering, good colonel, there's a woman in the case. No whispering.

BELVILE

(*aside to Blunt*). Hark'ee, fool, be advised, and conceal both the ring and the story for your reputation's sake. Do not let people know what despised cullies we English are.

WILLMORE.

Come, come, where's the wench? We'll see her; let her be what she will, we'll see her.

PEDRO.

Ay, ay, let us see her. I can soon discover whether she be of quality, or for your diversion.

BLUNT.
She's in Fred's custody.

WILLMORE.
Come, come the key –

To Frederick, who gives him the key. They are going.

BELVILE.
– Stay, gentlemen! (*Aside*) Yet if I hinder 'em, they shall discover all – Hold, let's go one at once. Give me the key.

WILLMORE.
Nay, hold there, colonel, I'll go first.

FREDERICK.
Nay, no dispute, Ned and I have the propriety of her.

WILLMORE.
Damn propriety! Then we'll draw cuts. (*Belvile goes to whisper to Willmore.*) Nay, no corruption, good colonel. Come, the longest sword carries her.

They all draw, forgetting Don Pedro being a Spaniard, had the longest.

(*Aside*) Pox of his Toledo, I had forgot that. (*To Pedro*) The wench is yours.

BLUNT.
I yield up my interest to you, sir.

FREDERICK.
Come, sir, I'll conduct you to the lady.

PEDRO.
Sure, 'tis some common carrion. She'd never haunt your house else. (*Peeps through the curtain.*) Ha, 'tis a hot, crafty queen, she is so eager to go to it, she's already naked. I'll have her.

Exit Pedro.

BELVILE.
(*aside*). To hinder him will certainly discover her. – Dost know, dull beast, what mischief thou hast done?

Willmore walking up and down, out of humour.

WILLMORE.
Ay, ay, to trust our fortune to lots! A devil on't, 'twas madness, that's the truth on't.

BELVILE.
Oh, intolerable sot –

Enter Florinda running, masked, Pedro after her.

FLORINDA
(*aside*). Good heaven defend me from discovery!

PEDRO.
'Tis but in vain to fly me; you're fallen to my lot . . .

BELVILE
(*aside*). How shall I bring her off?

WILLMORE
(*aside*). Why, what a pox, is not this my woman, the same I followed but now?

Pedro talking to Florinda, who walks up and down.

PEDRO.
Come, show your face: I know your business here.

FLORINDA
(*aside*). Good heaven, I fear he does indeed.

PEDRO.
Come, what bashful? Be you as kind as I know you meant to be when you entered here. S'life, she's goodly limbed. I'll have her.

WILLMORE.
But sir, perhaps the lady will not be imposed upon. Let her choose her man.

PEDRO.
Yea, I am better bred than not to leave her choice free. Leave off this pretended coyness and take your pick of five good fellows that are as eager for the act thou camest for as thou art apt to undergo it. Or if you will, take all of us and let me be first i' the file.

Enter Valeria, and is surprised at the sight of Don Pedro.

VALERIA
(*aside*). Don Pedro here! There's no avoiding him.

FLORINDA
(*aside*). Valeria!

VALERIA
(*to Pedro*). Oh, I have found you, sir! The strangest accident – if I had breath – to tell it.

PEDRO.
Speak! Is Florinda safe? Hellena well?

VALERIA.
Ay, ay, sir. Florinda is safe – (*Aside*) From any fears of you.

PEDRO.
Why, where's Florinda? Speak!

VALERIA.

She's fled away in the habit – of one of her pages, sir. But Callis thinks you may retrieve her yet, if you make haste away. She'll tell you, sir, the rest . . .

PEDRO.

Dishonourable girl, she has undone my aim – (*To Belvile*) Sir, you see my necessity of leaving you, and I hope you'll pardon it. My sister, I know, will make her flight to you; and if she do, I shall expect she should be rendered back.

BELVILE.

I shall consult my love and honour, sir.

Exit Pedro.

FLORINDA

(*to Valeria*). My dear preserver, let me embrace thee.

WILLMORE.

What the devil's all this?

BLUNT.

Mystery, by this light.

FLORINDA.

I tell you, sister, thou hast chosen a very beastly cavalier to mell with. And this fellow here's as brutish.

VALERIA.

Come, come, talk not, but make haste and get yourselves married quickly, for your brother will return again.

BELVILE.

I'm so surprised with fears and joys, so amazed to find you here in safety, I can scarce persuade my heart into a faith of what I see.

WILLMORE.

Hark'ee, colonel, is this that mistress who has cost you so many sighs, and me so many quarrels with you?

BELVILE.

It is – (*To Florinda*) Pray give him the honour of your hand.

WILLMORE

(*kneels and kisses her hand*). . . . Give me your pardon, too.

FLORINDA.

The friend to Belvile may command me anything.

WILLMORE

(*aside*). Death, would I might; 'tis a surpassing beauty.

BELVILE.

Boy, run and fetch a father instantly.

Exit Philippo.

FREDERICK.

So, now do I stand like a dog, and have not a syllable to plead my own cause with. By this hand, madam, I was never so thoroughly confounded before, nor shall I ever more dare look up with confidence, till you are pleased to pardon me.

FLORINDA.

Sir, I'll be reconciled to you on one condition; that you'll follow the example of your friend in marrying a maid that does not hate you, and whose fortune, I believe, will not be unwelcome to you.

FREDERICK.

Madam, had I no inclinations that way, I should obey your kind commands.

BELVILE.

Who, Fred marry? He has few inclinations for womankind.

FREDERICK.

Oh, I do not use to boast of my intrigues.

BELVILE.

Boast! Why thou dost nothing but boast.

FREDERICK.

I wish this lady would think me more modest a man.

VALERIA.

She would be sorry then, and not like you half so well. And I should be loath to break my word with you, which was, that if your friend and mine agreed, it should be a match between you and I. (*She gives him her hand.*)

FREDERICK.

Bear witness, colonel, 'tis a bargain. (*Kisses her hand.*)

BLUNT

(*to Florinda*). I have a pardon to beg, too; but 'adsheartlikins, I am so out of countenance that I'm a dog if I can say anything to purpose.

FLORINDA.

Sir, I heartily forgive you all – if I may have a cloak now.

BLUNT.

That's nobly said, sweet lady. – Belvile, prithee present her her ring again, for I find I have not courage to approach her myself. (*Gives him the ring; he gives it to Florinda.*)

Enter Philippo.

PHILIPPO.

Sir, I have brought the father that you sent for. He would know your purposes and craves you speak to him; for I know not why you sent for him, nor whether 'twas for a christening or a burying.

Exit Philippo.

BELVILE.

'Tis well. And now, my dear Florinda, let's fly to complete that mighty joy we have so long wished and sighed for. – Come Fred, you'll follow?

FREDERICK.

Your example, sir, 'twas ever my ambition in war, and must be so in love.

WILLMORE.

And must not I see this juggling knot tied?

BELVILE.

No, thou shalt do us better service and be our guard, lest Don Pedro's sudden return interrupt the ceremony.

WILLMORE.

Content; I'll secure this pass.

Exeunt Belvile, Florinda, Frederick and Valeria.
Re-enter Philippo.

PHILIPPO

(*to Blunt*). Sir, your tailor waits you in your chamber with a noble suit of clothes all made to your measures. I warrant 'tis a goodly.

BLUNT.

Some comfort yet: I shall not dance naked at the wedding.

PHILIPPO

(*to Willmore*). Sir, there's a lady without would speak to you. She's very fine, fair and eager too. I told her you were not at liberty.

WILLMORE.

Nay, bring her in; I dare not quit my post. This can be none but my pretty gypsy.

Exeunt Blunt and Philippo.

Scene xix

Enter Angellica in a masking habit and vizard. Willmore runs to her.

WILLMORE

(*to Angellica.*) I see you can follow as well as fly. Come, confess thyself the most malicious devil in nature; you think you have

done my business with Angellica –

ANGELLICA.

It is not done.

She draws a pistol and holds it to his breast.

WILLMORE.

Ha, 'tis not she! What art thou?

ANGELLICA.

One thou hast injured, and who comes to kill thee for't.

Pulls off her vizard.

WILLMORE.

Angellica!

ANGELLICA.

Yes, traitor! Does not thy guilty blood run shivering through thy veins?

WILLMORE.

Faith, no child. My blood keeps its old ebbs and flows still, and that usual heat too, that could oblige thee with a kindness, had I but opportunity.

ANGELLICA.

Devil! Dost wanton with my pain?

WILLMORE.

Hold, dear virago! Hold thy hand a little,
I am not now at leisure to be killed.
(*Aside.*) Death, I think she's in earnest.

ANGELLICA.

What have you, sir, to say? –
(*Aside, turning from him*)
                                        Nay, nay do not speak
For I know well
I should hear thee out,
Thoud'st talk away all that is brave about me
And I have vowed thy death by all that's sacred.

Follows him with the pistol to his breast.

WILLMORE.

Why then, there's an end of a proper handsome fellow,
That might 'a lived to have done good service yet.

ANGELLICA

(*pausingly*). Yet – I would give thee time for – penitence.

WILLMORE.

Faith, child, I thank God I have ever took care to lead a good, sober, hopeful life, and am of a religion that teaches me to believe that I shall depart in peace.

ANGELLICA.
Nay, Willmore, tell me first . . . tell me how many
Such poor believing fools thou hast undone?
How many hearts thou hast betrayed to ruin?

WILLMORE.
Why, as I think, no more nor less than you.

ANGELLICA.
You said you loved me.

WILLMORE.
So I did, that instant.

ANGELLICA.
And at that instant I gave you my heart.
I'd pride enough and love enough to think
That it could raise thy soul above the vulgar,
Nay, make you all soul too, and soft and constant.
Why did you lie and cheapen me? Alas,
I thought all men were born to be my slaves,
And wore my power like lightning in my eyes;
But when love held the mirror, that cruel glass
Reflected all the weakness of my soul;
My pride was turned to a submissive passion
And so I bowed, which I ne'er did before
To anyone or anything but heaven.
I thought that I had won you and that you
Would value me the higher for my folly.
But now I see you gave no more than dog lust,
Made me your spaniel bitch; and so I fell
Like a long-worshipped idol at the last
Perceived a fraud, a cheat, a bauble. Why
Didst thou destroy my too long fancied power?
Why didst thou give me oaths? Why didst thou kneel
And make me soft? Why, why didst thou enslave me?

WILLMORE.
Egad, I see thy heart is shrewdly nipped.

ANGELLICA.
Ah, sir, ah, sir, I yet had been content
To wear my chains with vanity and joy,
Hadst thou not broke those vows that put them on.

WILLMORE.
Broke my vows? Why, where hast thou lived? Amongst the
gods? For I never heard of mortal man that has not broke a
thousand vows.

ANGELLICA.
Oh, fie!

WILLMORE.
Angellica, thou has made a thousand lovers languish, who, in
the amorous fever, no doubt have sworn like me. Did they all
die in that faith, still adoring? I do not think they did.

ANGELLICA.
Had I repaid their vows, as I did thine
I would have killed them also that had spurned me.

WILLMORE.
This old general has quite spoiled thee: nothing makes a woman
so vain as being flattered. Your old lover ever supplies the
defects of age with intolerable dotage, vast charge, and that
which you call constancy; and attributing all this to your own
beauty, you domineer, and throw your favours in's teeth,
upbraiding him still with the defects of age, and cuckold him as
often as he deceives your expectations.

ANGELLICA.
All this is true, for which I hate thee more.

WILLMORE.
I wish I were that dull, that constant thing
Which thou wouldst have, and nature never meant me.
I must, like cheerful birds, sing in all groves,
And perch a little while on every bough
Billing the next kind she that flies to meet me;
Yet, after all, could build my nest with thee,
Thither repairing when I'd loved my round,
And still reserve a tributary flame.

ANGELLICA.
Ah sir, you have a charm almost persuades
Me to take you as you are, and not as I
Will have you be. And yet by god, I will not
Share you with any. I am one that would have
All or none. Therefore –

WILLMORE.
– Nay stay a while.
To gain my credit and to prove my faith
I'll pay you back your golden charity
And be obliged for nothing but for love.

ANGELLICA.
O that you were in earnest. Would you sought
To buy me still. So mean a thought of me
Would turn my present rage and pain to scorn.
And I should pity thee and let thee live;
Which for the public safety of our sex

Willmore, I will not do. Therefore, prepare.
I will no more be tempted with replies.

WILLMORE.

Sure –

ANGELLICA.

Damn thee! I've heard thee talk too long.

PHILIPPO

(*without*). You shall not win. She's with a gentleman.

Scene xx

Enter Don Antonio, his arm in a scarf, and lays hold on the pistol.

ANTONIO.

Ha! Angellica!

ANGELLICA.

Antonio! What devil brought thee hither?

ANTONIO.

Love and curiosity, seeing your coach at the door. Let me disarm you of this unbecoming instrument of death. (*Takes away the pistol.*) Amongst the number of your slaves was there not one worthy the honour to have fought your quarrel? – (*To Willmore*) Who are you sir, that are so very wretched to merit death from her? What pretensions have you to this lady?

WILLMORE.

One, sir, that could have made a better end of an amorous quarrel without you, than with you.

ANTONIO.

Sure 'tis the English rogue that took down her picture yesterday; yea, the very same that set on me last night! Blessed opportunity – (*Offers to shoot him.*)

ANGELLICA.

Hold, you're mistaken, sir.

ANTONIO.

By heaven, the very same!

WILLMORE.

Sir, I do not use to be examined, and am ill at all disputes but this – (*Draws; Antonio offers to shoot.*)

ANGELLICA

(*To Willmore*). Oh, hold! You see he's armed with certain death.

And you, Antonio, I command you hold

By all the passion you've so lately vowed me!

ANTONIO.

May you destroy me with your mortal hate
When I refuse obedience to your will.

Enter Don Pedro, sees Antonio, and stays.

By all that's holy, I adore you so,
That even my rival, who has charms enough
To make him fall a victim to my jealousy,
Shall live and shall have leave to love on still.

PEDRO

(*aside*). What's this I hear?

ANGELLICA.

                         Antonio, yesterday
I'd not have sold my interest in his heart
For all thy sword has won and lost in battle.

(*To Willmore*)

But now, to show my utmost of contempt,
I give thee life; which, if thou wouldst preserve,
Live where my eyes may never see thee more.
Live to undo someone whose soul may prove
So bravely constant to revenge my love.

(*To Antonio*)

Sir, since I have a thousand crowns of you,
Come to my chamber; when you will, I care not.

                                        Goes out.

Antonio follows, but Pedro pulls him back.

PEDRO.

Antonio, stay. Have you forgot Florinda?

ANTONIO.

Don Pedro!

PEDRO.

What coward fear was 't that prevented thee
From meeting me this morning on the Molo?

ANTONIO.

Meet thee?

PEDRO.

                         Yes, me, I was the man that dared thee.

ANTONIO.

(*laughs*). Finding myself unapt to use a sword
I send another blade to do thee right.

PEDRO.
But 'twas Florinda's quarrel that we fought.
And you, to show how little you esteemed her
Sent me your rival, Belvile in your place.
But I have found the cause of this affront,
And when I meet you fit for the dispute,
I'll tell you my resentment.

ANTONIO.
I shall be ready, sir, ere long, to do you reason.

Exit Antonio.

PEDRO.
If I could find Florinda, now whilst my anger's high, I think I should be kind, and give her to Belvile in revenge.

WILLMORE.
Faith, sir, I believe the priest within has been so kind.

PEDRO.
How? My sister married?

WILLMORE.
I hope by this time she is, and bedded too.

PEDRO.
Dares he do this? Does he not fear my power?

WILLMORE.
Faith, not at all.

PEDRO.
Who art thou?

WILLMORE.
One whose power's greater in this house than yours. I have a damned surly crew here that will keep you till the next tide, and then clap you on board for prize. My ship lies but a league off the Molo, and we shall show your donship a damned English rover's trick.

They draw. Enter Bevile.

BELVILE.
This rogue's in some new mischief. Ha! Pedro returned!

PEDRO.
Colonel Belvile, I hear you have married my sister.

BELVILE.
You have heard truth then, sir.

PEDRO.
Have I so? Then, sir, I wish you joy.

BELVILE.
How?

PEDRO.
By this embrace I do, and I am glad on't.

BELVILE.
Are you in earnest?

PEDRO.
By our long friendship and my obligations to thee, I am. I love my sister and shall with all honour endeavour to make her happy. You are fitter for her than Antonio. Come, lead me to my sister, that she may know I now approve her choice.

Exit Belvile with Pedro.

Enter Philippo.

PHILIPPO.
Sir, another lady's come, a reverent and a holy.

WILLMORE.
And what have I to do with such a one?

PHILIPPO.
She is importunate.

WILLMORE.
Then she wants money. Get her hence away.

PHILIPPO.
Nay, she's here already, sir, I'll leave you.

Goes.

Scene xxi

Enter Hellena, in the habit of a novice, which she wore at first.

WILLMORE.
Ha! My gypsy! Egad child, I was e'en in despair of ever seeing thee again; my friends are all provided for within, each man his kind woman. I was e'en resolved to go abroad, and condemn myself to a lone cabin, and the thoughts of thee.

HELLENA.
And could you have left me behind?

WILLMORE.
Why, 'twould have broke my heart, child.

HELLENA.
I beseech ye your name.

WILLMORE.

I am called Robert the Constant.

HELLENA.

A very fine name! Pray was it your falconer or boson that christened you? Do they not use to whistle when they call you?

WILLMORE.

I hope you have a better, you are so merry with mine.

HELLENA.

I am called Hellena the Inconstant. But, sir, since methinks your friends and mine are all provided for, will you be a faithful friend to me now? Or shall I back behind a grate again?

WILLMORE.

Nay, thou wert made for earth, child, not for heaven. Yet for being a friend I cannot promise: thou art of a form so excellent, a face and humour too good for cold, dull friendship. I am parlously afraid of being in love, child, and you have not forgotten how severely you have used me?

HELLENA.

That's all one; such usage you must still look for; to find out all your haunts, to rail at you before all that love you, till I have made you love only me in your own defence, because nobody else will love you.

WILLMORE.

Egad, I was never clawed away with such broadsides from any female before. Thou hast one virtue I adore – good nature.

HELLENA.

Nay, then, let's lose no time –

WILLMORE.

My time's as precious to me as thine can be. Therefore, dear creature, since we are so well agreed, let's retire to my chamber. Come, my bed's prepared for such a guest all clean and sweet as thy fair self. Come, let's retire and fall to.

HELLENA.

'Tis but getting my consent, and the business is soon done. Let but old gaffer Hymen and his priest say amen to't, and I dare lay my mother's daughter by as proper a fellow as your father's son, without fear or blushing.

WILLMORE.

Hold, hold, no bug words, child. Priest and Hymen? No, no, we'll have no vows but love, child. Marriage is as certain a bane to love as lending money is to friendship. I'll neither ask nor give another vow, though I could be content to have the pleasure of working that great miracle of making a maid a mother, if you durst venture.

HELLENA.

And what shall I get? A cradle full of noise and mischief, with a pack of repentance at my back? Can you teach me to weave swaddling clothes to pass my time with?

WILLMORE.

I can teach thee to weave a true love's knot better.

HELLENA.

So can my dog.

WILLMORE.

Well, I see we are both upon our guards, and I see there's no way to conquer good nature but by yielding. Here, give me thy hand: one kiss, and I am thine.

HELLENA.

One kiss! How like my page he speaks! I am resolved you shall have none, for asking such a sneaking sum. Good friend single-kiss, is all your talking come to this? A kiss, a caudle! I'll to my nunnery. Farewell, captain single-kiss.

Going out. He stays her.

WILLMORE.

By heaven, both the Indies shall not buy thee from me. I adore thy humour and will marry thee, and we are so of one humour it must be a bargain. Give me thy hand. (*Kisses her hand.*) And now let the blind ones, love and fortune, do their worst.

HELLENA.

Why, god-a-mercy, captain!

Scene xxii

Enter Pedro, Belvile, Florinda, Frederick and Valeria.

PEDRO.

Ha! Hellena!

FLORINDA.

Hellena!

HELLENA.

The very same. Ha! My brother! Now, captain, show your love and courage; stand to your arms and defend me bravely, or I am lost forever.

PEDRO.

What's this I hear? False girl, how came you hither, and what's your business? Speak!

Goes roughly to her.

WILLMORE.

Hold off, sir; you have leave to parley only.

Puts himself between.

HELLENA.

Faith, brother, my business is the same with all living creatures of my age: to love and be beloved – and here's the man.

PEDRO.

Hast thou deceived me too; deceived thyself and heaven?

HELLENA.

Be you but kind, let me alone with heaven.

PEDRO.

Belvile, I did not expect this false play from you. Was't not enough you'd gain Florinda, which I pardoned, but your lewd friends too must be enriched with the spoils of a noble family? (*Sees Valeria with Frederick.*) What, all three ruined in an instant?

BELVILE.

Faith, sir, I am as much surprised at this as you can be. Yet, sir, my friends are gentlemen, and ought to be esteemed for their misfortunes, since they have the glory to suffer with the best of men and kinds. 'Tis true, he's a rover of fortune, yet a prince aboard his little wooden world.

PEDRO.

What's that to me?

FLORINDA.

We three have consulted nature and reason, brother, and find from neither that right of Empire that brothers claim over sisters, or fathers over daughters. And since we doubt not that in this carnival thou hast enjoyed those advantages that strength and custom gives you over our sex, 'tis both justice and wisdom in us to have done likewise.

PEDRO.

Sister, that's cant. (*To Willmore*) But can you maintain a woman of Hellena's birth and fortune?

WILLMORE.

Faith, sir, I can boast of nothing but a sword which does me right where'er I come and since I loved her before I either knew her birth or name, I must pursue my resolution and marry her.

PEDRO.

And is all your holy intent of becoming a nun debauched into a desire of man?

HELLENA.

Why, I have considered the matter, brother, and find the three

hundred thousand crowns my uncle left me, and you cannot keep from me, will be better laid out in love than in religion.

BELVILE.

Let most voices carry it; for heaven or the captain?

ALL CRY.

A captain! A captain!

HELLENA.

Look ye, sir, 'tis a clear case.

PEDRO.

Oh, I am mad! – (*Aside*) If I refuse, my life's in danger – Take her: I shall now be free from fears of her honour. Guard it you now, if you can; I have been a slave to't long enough.

Gives her to him.

WILLMORE.

Faith, sir, I am of a nation that are of the opinion a woman's honour is not worth guarding when she has a mind to part with it.

HELLENA.

Well said, captain.

PEDRO.

(*to Valeria*). This was your plot, mistress.

VALERIA.

There's no altering destiny, sir.

PEDRO.

Sooner than a woman's will. Therefore I forgive you all, and wish you may get my father's pardon as easily, which I fear.

Enter Blunt dressed in a Restoration habit, looking very ridiculously; Philippo adjusting his band.

PHILIPPO.

'Tis very well, sir. I ne'er saw you look so fine.

BLUNT.

Well, sir! 'Adsheartlikins, I tell you 'tis damnable ill, sir. A Spanish habit! Good lord! Could the devil and my tailor devise no other punishment for me but the mode of a nation I abominate?

BELVILE.

What's the matter, Ned?

BLUNT.

Pray view me round, and judge. (*Turns round.*)

BELVILE.

I must confess thou art a kind of an odd figure.

BLUNT.
I had rather be in the Inquisition for Judaism than in this doublet and breeches. Methinks I look like a bouquet garni stuffed full of fool's flesh.

BELVILE.
Methinks 'tis well, and makes thee look e'en cavalier.

WILLMORE.
Come, sir, settle your face and salute your friends.

BLUNT.
Ha! Sayst thou so, my little rover? (*To Hellena*) Lady, if you be one, give me leave to kiss your hand, and tell you, 'adsheartlikins, for all I look so, I am your humble servant.

Carnival music is heard.

WILLMORE
(*to Hellena*). Come, we'll to the good man within, who stays to give us a cast of his office. Have you no trembling at the near approach?

HELLENA.
No more than you have in an engagement or a tempest.

WILLMORE.
Egad, thou'rt a brave girl, and I admire thy love and courage.

Willmore and Hellena go in.

FREDERICK.
Hark! What's this?

BELVILE.
'Tis a custom of my country.

PHILIPPO.
The gay people in masquerade, who make every man's house their own, are coming up. Pray, let 'em enter, for they're merry.

Enter Masquers with music and dancing.

BLUNT.
'Adsheartlikins, would 'twere lawful to pull off their false faces, that I might see if my doxy were not amongst 'em.

BELVILE.
Nay, let's have no more banging. (*To the Masquers*) Ladies and gentlemen, since you are come so apropos, you must drink with us ere Lent be come.

They sit and drink. The music changes.

BELVILE.
I'll give you all a toast. To the Prince over the water.

They drink a toast with English music. A bell sounds for the beginning of Lent.

So now each one of you must back to's several occupations.

All shed their Carnival gear, the Masquers all appearing as slaves and such like, and go out singing a working song.

FLORINDA.
And must thou back to thine?

BELVILE.
                    Yea for a little.

FLORINDA.
Alas.

BELVILE.
Soon shall the King be set upon his throne
Then all to England shall enjoy their own.
But let us now no future dangers dread
Than present ventures of the marriage bed.

Exeunt to music of the Restoration.